The Articulate Classroom

Talking and Learning in the Primary School

Edited by

Prue Goodwin

David Fulton Publishers

London

David Fulton Publishers Ltd
Ormond House, 26–27 Boswell Street, London WC1N 3JZ

www.fultonpublishers.co.uk

First published in Great Britain by David Fulton Publishers 2001

Note: The right of Prue Goodwin to be identified as the editor of this work has been asserted by her in accordance with the Copyright, Designs and Patents Act 1988.

Copyright © David Fulton Publishers Ltd 2001

British Library Cataloguing in Publication Data
A catalogue record for this book is available from the British Library

ISBN 1–85346–703–0

The publishers would like to thank John Cox for copy-editing and Sheila Harding for proofreading this book.

Typeset by FiSH Books, London
Printed by The Cromwell Press Ltd, Trowbridge, Wilts.

Contents

Contributors

Lesley Clark is a lecturer in Language and Education at the Reading and Language Information Centre, The University of Reading. She was previously a teacher in primary schools in England and Singapore, working with all ages of pupils but particularly with early years. Her book *Help Your Child with Reading* (Hodder & Stoughton 1994) offers guidance to parents about supporting their children's literacy learning.

Lyn Dawes has been a primary science coordinator at a school in Milton Keynes and a teacher-researcher for the Open University. She has published widely in the field of speaking and listening in the primary school. Lyn has been involved with initial teacher education at De Montfort University and is currently Education Officer for the British Educational Communications and Technology Agency (BECTA).

Janet Evans was a primary school teacher before becoming a senior lecturer in education at Liverpool Hope University College. She has written many books and articles on education and has travelled widely as part of her work and continues to work in schools carrying out action research with primary pupils and their educators.

Julia Gillen is a Senior Research Fellow at the Institute of Education, The Manchester Metropolitan University. She has published on child development, qualitative research methodologies and the work of Vygotsky. Recently she has co-authored a multimedia training resource *Shaping the Future: Training to work with the under threes*.

Prue Goodwin taught in primary and middle schools for over twenty years before becoming an advisory teacher and then Lecturer in Language and Director of INSET at the Reading and Language Information Centre, The University of Reading. She also contributes to the MA in Children's Literature at the University of Surrey Roehampton.

Judith Graham lectures at The University of Surrey Roehampton, London and also at the School of Education in Cambridge. She entered teacher education in the late 1970s after teaching in London comprehensive schools. She is the author of *Pictures on the Page* (NATE 1990), *Cracking Good Books* (NATE 1997) and co-editor with Alison Kelly of *Reading Under Control* and *Writing Under Control* (both David Fulton Publishers 1998).

Teresa Grainger is a principal lecturer at Canterbury Christ Church University College. Although most of her time is spent in teacher education, she still teaches regularly in classrooms, where her particular interests are in the language arts – especially drama, storytelling and children's literature. Her published work includes *Practical Storytelling in the Primary Classroom* (Scholastic 1997), *Resourcing drama 5–8* and *Resourcing drama 8–14* with Mark Cremin (NATE 2000) and *Inclusive Educational Practice: Literacy* with Janet Tod (David Fulton Publishers 2000).

Elizabeth Grugeon is Senior Lecturer in English in Primary Education at De Monfort University, where she teaches English specialists on the Primary BEd degree course. She is particularly interested in children's literature, language development and oral culture. She is a co-author of *Teaching Speaking and Listening in the Primary School* (David Fulton Publishers 1999) and *The Art of Storytelling for Teachers and Pupils: using stories to develop literacy in Primary Classrooms* (David Fulton Publishers 2000).

George Hunt taught in several London primary schools and has worked on literacy programmes in Dominica and Mongolia. He is currently a Lecturer in Language in Education at The University of Reading. His publications include *Inspirations for grammar* (Scholastic 1994) and *Curriculum Bank: Reading at Key Stage 2* (Scholastic 1995). He is a regular contributor to *Books for Keeps* magazine.

Andy Kempe lectures at The University of Reading where he leads the secondary PGCE course for drama specialists and provides courses for teachers working in all phases of education. He has been particularly involved with helping primary teachers find the links between drama and literacy, especially the integration of dramatic texts into the drama curriculum. He has published widely on drama and drama teaching.

Jackie Kirk was a primary teacher in London before she became a teacher educator in Montreal, working with preservice teachers in the Faculty of Education at McGill University. She also works with practising teachers as a consultant in schools. Jackie is involved in research in teacher education and international development, recently working at the University of Witswatersrand, South Africa, in Niger and southern India.

Michael Lockwood taught in schools for eight years before becoming a Lecturer in English and Education at The University of Reading. His publications include *Opportunities for English in the Primary School* (Trentham 1996), *Practical ways to teach standard English and language study, Poetry in and out of the literacy hour* and *Drama in and out of the literacy hour* (all three published by the Reading and Language Information Centre, The University of Reading).

Sue Lyle taught in primary schools before becoming a teacher educator at Swansea Institute of Higher Education. Her research interests focus on the investigation of children's collaborative talk, on which she has published widely. As director of the Master's programme, she actively supports practising teachers wishing to research in the field of speaking and listening.

Joy McCormick works with the Education Development Unit, St Martin's College, Lancaster. Working in partnership with schools and LEAs, she has been involved in many school improvement projects, developing effective practice in teaching and learning. She is committed to working alongside teachers and children in schools in order to encourage reflective and positive literacy learning.

Frank Monaghan is an EAL teacher in North Westminster Community School in London, where he is also the Literacy and Numeracy Coordinator. He was seconded to work at the Reading and Language Information Centre, The University of Reading, as senior research fellow on the Fabula Project.

David Skidmore is a lecturer in education in the Department of Education at the University of Bath. He has published widely on education and has just completed *Inclusion: The Dynamic of School Development*, to be published by Open University Press in 2001. David leads courses on inclusive education and disability rights in education.

Carol Smith has been a primary teacher and English coordinator for many years. She is currently a literacy consultant working for Milton Keynes Learning and Development Directorate. Carol is also a visiting lecturer at the University of Hertfordshire and De Montfort University.

Introduction
Prue Goodwin

Talking is such an every day activity that we seldom take much notice of it. But imagine a day without it. Even someone who lives alone is unlikely to escape the spoken word as they travel to work, pop into the shops or switch on the television. Most of us spend much of the day speaking to a range of audiences (e.g. partners, children, shopkeepers), for a range of purposes (greeting, explaining, complaining). Those of us engaged in teaching are involved with talk all day, whether as social interaction or with the exploratory talk that goes on whenever learning is taking place. Talk involves both speaking and listening. When we speak we shape our thoughts into meanings. The listener hears and unravels our meanings before they reply. But the functions served by spoken language are far more wide reaching than individuals communicating with each other. Looking at talk in its widest use we can see that it is the means by which:

- Each of us explore what we think and how we feel. It is human nature to tell others about important events in our lives, whether it is to share pleasures or to seek support. In extremes of emotion – distress, confusion or grief – we turn to counsellors, psychiatrists and spiritual advisers to help us. By talking through problems we begin to gain control over them and understand how best to overcome them.
- We understand and maintain comfortable human relationships. The relationships can be with our closest family and friends or at the level of international diplomacy. Keeping channels of communication open can resolve a squabble on the playground or prevent an international war.
- Society organises itself. Government in the UK works through discussion in committees and meetings as well as through the great debates in the House of Commons. The word parliament originates from the French *parler* – to speak, and a good orator is sometimes considered, rightly or wrongly, a good politician.

With talk, in all its various forms, being so central to all aspects of our lives, it is essential that children are given opportunities to become confident speakers and listeners. The programme of study for speaking and listening in the National Curriculum for English (DfEE/QCA 1999) indicates the importance attached to children gaining an understanding of oracy. In this book teachers, advisors and educational researchers have contributed chapters that consider good practice in teaching speaking and listening and have offered highly relevant contributions to an overall understanding of the place of exploratory talk in primary schools.

Talk in the primary curriculum

In the children's novel *Charlie Lewis Plays for Time* by Gene Kemp (1986), a supply teacher, Mr Carter, decides to get back to basics with the class. Charlie and his friend, Trish, find it all rather tedious:

> I sat down where our Group A was silently working its way through oh, no, not again, *New and Improved English for Primary Schools*.
>
> 'D'you remember when we did it over and over in Mrs Somers' class?' muttered Trish, shooting down the page at the speed of light.
>
> 'Quiet there. This is a language lesson so there should be no talking AT ALL.'
>
> After a minute, 'You should see what the rest have got. *Reading for Finding Out* and *Fun with Word Families*,' hissed Trish. I just wished she'd belt up and let us get on with it in quiet miserable boredom. Too late.
>
> 'Table A will stay on to work at break as they are apparently incapable of maintaining an orderly silence.'

In the 1960s, many primary teachers would have shared Mr Carter's views about talking in class. However, from that time onwards, the influence of educationalists and linguists such as James Britton (1970) and Joan Tough (1976) changed the commonly held idea that silent classrooms were educationally successful classrooms. Their work highlighted the pivotal role talk plays in learning, and focused attention on the need for all teachers to understand how to provide for a previously neglected aspect of their pupils' learning potential. In this chapter, we will look at how talk slowly gained in standing in the primary curriculum and ask what are the characteristics of an articulate classroom in a primary school.

Forty years of evolution

Despite the widespread knowledge of the importance of talk, modification of practice in schools has been very gradual. Back in the 1960s, teachers who associated talking with wasting time may have feared that classes would be full of chattering rather than purposeful conversations leading to enhanced levels of understanding across the curriculum. A change in terminology eventually imbued talk with a status much closer to that of literacy:

> in a set of papers (1965), … Andrew Wilkinson first formulated the term 'oracy', a term analogous to literacy as a prerequisite for successful learning. Synthesising the findings of linguistics and cognitive psychology, the argument was that learners need to learn through talk, particularly through working co-operatively in small groups.
>
> (Keiner 1992)

The Bullock report, *A Language for Life* (DES 1975), gave official backing for the view that talking and listening was an essential part of schooling: 'Exploratory talk by pupils has an important function in the process of learning'. Throughout the next ten years, although the Schools' Council (1979) had advocated greater emphasis on talk in schools, there was little noticeable change in classroom practice. By 1988, the year of the Education Act that led to the creation of the National Curriculum, talk in schools had still failed to make a major impact.

> A high proportion of classroom activity involves talk of two kinds: the teacher explaining while pupils listen and answer the odd closed question; and the pupils

chattering in a non-purposeful way. This is not always disruptive, but neither is it
fruitful.   (Jones 1988)

However, change was on its way in the form of a government funded initiative. The
need for children to talk about their thinking, their learning and the classroom activities
they engaged in as an essential part of every school day was firmly established in teachers' minds by the work of the National Oracy Project (NOP). Knowledge of the centrality
of talk in education was no longer confined to groups of pioneering teachers in isolated
projects across the country; it was 'being addressed by thousands of teachers in a variety of exploratory and innovative ways' (Wells 1992). The results of the NOP research
and dissemination to teachers were to be crucial in bringing about important changes in
practice in the following few years.

The NOP clearly exerted an influence on the 1989 National Curriculum for English
which had a whole section on oracy. Many colleagues interpreted the inclusion of
speaking and listening as a requirement to ensure children spoke 'properly'. But the
document challenged this interpretation with statements, such as:

> Primary schools must respect children's talk, as children put into words their thoughts
> and feelings, explore new ideas and deepen understanding. Teachers act as enablers
> by the use of skilled and open-ended questioning in order to lead the child to clarity
> of thought and expression.   (DES/WO 1989, para. 3.6)

Through all its revisions, the National Curriculum for English emphasised the place of
speaking and listening as a separate aspect of the language curriculum. In *English in the
National Curriculum* (DFE 1995) the programme of study contained little more than lists
of items to be covered. However, reflected in the lists was the continued commitment
to the role of talk in learning:

> Pupils should be given opportunities to talk for a range of purposes, including:
>
> - exploring, developing, and explaining ideas
> - planning, predicting, and investigating;
> - sharing ideas, insights and opinions.   (DfEE 1995)

Oracy and the National Literacy Strategy

The next significant government initiative in this area was the National Literacy Project,
implemented by the fading Conservative government in 1996 and transformed into the
National Literacy Strategy (NLS) by New Labour in 1997. The emphasis on raising standards in reading and writing might well have had the effect of relegating oracy to the
position of a mere adjunct of literacy. However, this did not prove to be the case.

The lack of explicit reference to speaking and listening in the 1998 *Framework for
teaching* may well have led some colleagues to believe there would be a return to the
days so longed for by Mr Carter in *Charlie Lewis Plays for Time*. However, if anything,
fulfilling the guidance of the *Framework* requires more talk in classrooms rather than
less. The *Framework* itself points out that: 'The most successful teaching is: discursive –
characterised by high quality oral work; interactive – pupils' contributions are encouraged, expected and extended' (DfEE 1998). The concise style of this statement might be
expanded into the following rather more meaningful interpretation: good practice is
about purposeful and genuine conversations between teachers and pupils. Shared and
guided reading and writing are entirely about talking through the literacy task in hand,

and, whether children are responding to books, discussing words or contributing during plenary sessions, oracy is at the heart of the literacy hour.

It should be noted, however, that the accompanying advice to schools about organising group discussion fails to acknowledge the need for exploratory talk (see Chapter 6 by George Hunt). It could also be argued that the *Framework* and NLS in-service training pack do not make the importance of talk clear. That said, it is unlikely that anything on the lists of things that children 'should be taught' term by term can be achieved successfully without a great deal of talk. It is unfortunate that this message has not always seemed to get across clearly to schools, or even to LEA advisors.

Speaking and listening in the new National Curriculum

With the coming of the latest revision of the National Curriculum (1999), the programme of study for speaking and listening emphasises the development of social skills almost to the exclusion of the cognitive. The list for Key Stage 2, for example, reads:

Pupils should be taught:

- To speak with confidence in a range of contexts, adapting their speech for a range of purposes and audiences.
- To listen, understand and respond appropriately to others.
- To talk effectively as members of a group.
- To participate in a wide range of drama activities and to evaluate their own and other's contributions.
- The grammatical constructions that are characteristic of spoken standard English and apply this knowledge appropriately in a range of contexts.
- About how language varies:
  - according to context and purpose
  - between standard and dialect forms
  - between spoken and written forms.

All of these statements clearly have a strong social focus. Consider, for example, the chief purpose of group discussion and interaction where most cognitive talk is likely to take place. Children are expected to 'talk effectively as members of a group', stressing turn taking, dealing politely with opposing views, taking different roles (e.g. chair, scribe, spokesperson) and helping to move the group forward. There is a mention of making 'exploratory and tentative comments where ideas are being collected together' (DfEE/QCA 1999), however, there is little recognition of the way learners work on their own understanding by talking through learning tasks.

This lack of explicit direction in the English Order concerning the central role of exploratory talk may possibly be explained by the fact that greater recognition is given to talk across the entire curriculum, not just English. Yet even where the cross curricula use of language is described, again the social rather than cognitive aspects of talk are emphasised. Take for example the exhortation set out in the discussion of 'Use of language across the curriculum' that: 'In speaking, pupils should be taught to use language precisely and cogently' (DfEE/QCA 1999, p. 38) which implies that the needs of listeners should be uppermost in speakers' minds. The exploratory nature of cognitive talk might be seen to be in conflict with the social demands of being 'precise and cogent'. It is difficult to disentangle the actual intentions of the QCA. On the one hand, the main documents stress social over cognitive aspects of talk while on the other hand, supplementary materials such as *Teaching Speaking and Listening in Key Stages 1 and 2*

(QCA 1999), state that: 'Children's ability to speak and to listen is fundamental to their language development, learning in school, and to social development'. The position taken in this book is that primary teachers must plan to accommodate both the cognitive and the social dimensions of talk. Both are important but, it could be argued that, if anything, cognitive talk deserves greater emphasis. As Douglas Barnes points out, cognitive talk is vital and most successful where learners are socially equipped to share their learning with each other:

> The readiest way of working on understanding is often through talk, because the flexibility of speech makes it easy for us to try out new ways of arranging what we know, and easy too to change them if they seem inadequate. Of particular importance is the fact that we can talk to one another, collaborating and trying out our new ways of thinking.
> (Barnes 1992, p. 125)

Creating an articulate classroom

With government legislation and other pressures from outside the classroom, it is easy for primary teachers to be more concerned about covering the content of the speaking and listening curriculum than thinking about how best to achieve it. The very nature of talk – being transitory and accommodating of any context – makes a definition of an articulate classroom almost impossible, but some characteristics can be clearly observed in classrooms where it is evident that talk is an effective part of learning. There are, of course, certain basic necessities, such as ensuring that children can hear each other and that the room is arranged (or easily adaptable) to be conducive to talk. But beyond the organisation of furniture, an articulate classroom is one where:

- all voices are valued;
- talk is part of the whole curriculum;
- creativity and imagination are encouraged;
- language itself is talked about.

Everyone has a voice and all voices are valuable

No matter what your age, joining in with a discussion requires confidence. If for any reason you feel your voice is out of place or that your views are unimportant, you are unlikely to open your mouth. In the primary classroom everyone's contribution is significant and no one should be made to feel that they are excluded. Of course, there are some children who are naturally quiet or have special needs but Liz Grugeon (Chapter 1) reminds us that the classroom is not the only place in school where children converse. You only have to listen to the children in their own social groups to discover the genuinely reticent talkers. Pupils bring with them to the classroom the discourse of the playground. It reflects their immediate experiences and concerns as well as their individual voices.

Although there may be a place for considering how and why spoken standard English is used in certain social circumstances, insisting on 'correct' speech during any learning task or Circle Time will not empower children to speak with confidence or to take risks when making speculations. All children must feel that the content of what they say is important. Anxiety about how they sound should not be an issue.

Children will feel more confident and secure when their languages are valued and respected than when they are ignored or treated with contempt. Acceptance of linguistic diversity is an essential feature of all good educational practice.

(Edwards 1995, p. 7)

Once in the classroom, a great deal of time will be spent asking and answering questions. When teachers seek opinions, speculations or explanations from their pupils, it is important that children feel secure about speaking out and giving genuine answers. David Skidmore (Chapter 2) compares two different classroom conversations and suggests which approach supports children most successfully. Children need both structured and unstructured opportunities to talk freely in the classroom. Circle Time (Carol Smith, Chapter 3) provides a safe environment for youngsters to speak openly to each other about their concerns. On other occasions learners may appear to be talking to themselves, or at least for themselves, as they struggle to articulate their learning (Chapter 4). In the well-organised primary classroom the wide variety of speaking and listening opportunities will be enhanced by all the languages, dialects and accents that are represented. Apart from anything else, such a celebration of diversity offers a fertile starting point for talking about language.

Talk is part of the whole curriculum

Although speaking and listening comes within the requirements for teaching English, oracy is an essential tool of learning for any subject. Judith Graham (Chapter 5), George Hunt (Chapter 6) and Joy McCormick (Chapter 7) describe how oracy supports reading and writing. Sue Lyle (Chapter 8) demonstrates how talk about the classification of information helps children link new knowledge to old as they learn about the world around them. The activities with singing, re-enacting and playing with dolls that very young pupils undertook with Janet Evans (Chapter 9) led to valuable experiences with mathematical concepts. Talking through learning and articulating methods of working out maths problems are fundamental to the advice given in the National Numeracy Strategy (DfEE 1999). It is likewise recognised that work at the computer encourages lively exploratory talk. Lyn Dawes, Michael Lockwood and Frank Monaghan (Chapters 10, 16 and 17 respectively) all reinforce the value of children talking over their learning when computers are involved.

Creativity and imagination

Sound primary practice has always employed the learning power of creativity. Although it may not be immediately apparent in documents such as the NLS *Framework* and National Curriculum, there is an implicit assumption that children will be using their imagination and engaging in creative tasks in all subjects. Speaking and listening are no exception. In Chapter 11, Lesley Clark points out the range of talk that goes on in the early years classroom, much of it involving playing with language, role play and other creative activities. As James Britton pointed out:

The talk that goes along with the activities ... is essential to learning, and it is a direct continuation of the small child's talk in his family. In due course, moreover, writing will grow from that talk: I do not mean to suggest that it comes without effort on the part of the child or the teacher, but their efforts are directed towards that growth from those roots.

(Britton 1970)

Although the new curriculum document pays less attention to the cognitive functions of talk than in previous ones, it increases the emphasis on the place of drama – especially role play – when teaching the speaking and listening programmes of study. From the very early years, engaging in imagined experience assists children to express themselves. In the nursery classroom Julia Gillen observed children holding 'conversations' on the telephone in the role play area (Chapter 12). Their behaviour not only revealed the influence of the language children hear around them but also demonstrated how such imaginative play enabled even the very young to extend their linguistic resources. As children get older, improvising in a variety of imagined situations can require quite sophisticated discussion about how to talk in social contexts. As Andy Kempe (Chapter 13) points out, children can become involved in thinking about register, vocabulary and presentation as they take part in drama activities.

Listening to and telling stories is a time-honoured means of teaching and learning. It is almost impossible to over emphasise the importance of storytelling in school. Teresa Grainger (Chapter 14) for instance, highlights how stories support learning, especially literacy learning. Creating and writing stories collaboratively can be a whole-class or small group activity. Either way it will support children's growing skills with writing. In Chapter 15 Jackie Kirk describes how the telling and writing of a story in a multilingual classroom led to all sorts of benefits, not least the increased self-esteem of children for whom English was an additional language.

Talking about language

Use of speaking and listening will be enhanced by knowing more about the spoken word. Knowledge about language enables us to reflect on its use, adapt according to context and become more competent language users. Much is known about how groups of talkers operate, the roles taken on by individuals – whether consciously or not – and the influence on outcomes of attitudes and behaviour. How we talk together will affect the quality of any outcomes.

> Children may never have thought about how they talk together or consider whether different ways of communicating might make group activities more productive and enjoyable. They need help to learn how to use language effectively.
>
> (Dawes *et al.* 2000)

In classes where talk is valued and children are encouraged to contribute to a range of discussions, pupils soon discover for themselves the frustrations of disorganised argument. Lyn Dawes (Chapter 16) describes how children set about structuring their talk to ensure that everyone gets an equal chance to contribute. Children engaged in Circle Time (Carol Smith, Chapter 3) have also reflected on how to organise their communal sessions to enable all to take part. It is easier to understand about appropriate language use if, for example, children have discussed the reasons why we adapt our voices in different social situations. Literacy learning also requires time to reflect on language use. Michael Lockwood's research reinforces the value of talk at the computer as he describes the way youngsters discuss grammar in their writing when using a word processor (Chapter 17).

An articulate classroom

An articulate classroom is a community of learners and teachers who share an understanding about the roles of talk in their learning and the many social contexts they experience. Oracy, like literacy, will both be part of every subject area and a subject in its own right. The languages heard in the room will reflect all the different tongues and dialects used by the children and every child's voice will carry equal value. Children will feel secure enough to say what they think, to take risks with their learning and to let their imagination feed their understanding.

References

Barnes, D. (1992) 'The role of talk in learning', in Norman, K. (ed.) *Thinking voices: the work of the National Oracy Project*, 125. Sevenoaks: Hodder & Stoughton.

Britton, J. (1970) *Language and Learning*. Harmondsworth: Penguin.

Dawes, L., Mercer, N. and Wegerif, R. (2000) *Thinking Together*. Birmingham: The Questions Publishing Company.

Department For Education (1995) *English in the National Curriculum*. London: HMSO.

Department For Education and Employment (DfEE) (1998) *National Literacy Strategy Framework for Teaching*. London: DfEE.

Department For Education and Employment and the Qualifications and Curriculum Authority (DfEE/QCA) (1999) *The National Curriculum Handbook for teachers in England*. London: HMSO.

Department of Education and Science (DES) (1975) *A Language for Life*. (The Bullock Report.) London: HMSO.

DfEE (1999) *The National Numeracy Strategy: Framework for teaching mathematics from Reception to Year 6*. London: DfEE.

Department of Education and Science and the Welsh Office (DES/WO) (1989) *English in the National Curriculum*. London: HMSO.

Edwards, V. (1995) *Speaking and Listening in Multilingual Classrooms*. Reading: Reading and Language Information Centre.

Jones, P. (1988) *Lipservice: the Story of Talk in Schools*. Milton Keynes: Open University Press.

Keiner, J. (1992) 'A brief history of the origins of the National Oracy Project', in Norman, K. (ed.) *Thinking Voices: the work of the National Oracy Project*, 247–55. Sevenoaks: Hodder & Stoughton.

Kemp, G. (1986) *Charlie Lewis Plays for Time*. Harmondsworth: Puffin Books.

Qualifications and Curriculum Authority (QCA) (1999) *Teaching Speaking and Listening in Key Stages 1 and 2*. London: QCA.

Schools' Council (1979) *Learning through talk 11–16*. Working Paper 64. London: Evans.

Tough, J. (1976) *Listening to Children Talking*. London: Ward Lock Education/Drake Education Associates.

Wells, G. (1992) 'The centrality of talk in education', in Norman, K. (ed.) *Thinking Voices: the work of the National Oracy Project*, 283–310. Sevenoaks: Hodder & Stoughton.

Part 1

Every voice is valued

Chapter 1

The articulate playground –
Trainee teachers meet pocket monsters
Elizabeth Grugeon

> The scraps of lore which children learn from each other are at once more real, more immediately serviceable, and more vastly entertaining than anything which they learn from grownups.
>
> (Opie, I. and P. 1959, p. 1)

> For the most part teachers fail to capitalise on the wealth of material informally learned by children within the traditional culture of the playground... (Widdowson 2000)

In March 2000, 70 trainee primary school teachers in their third year of a BEd degree at De Montfort University were asked to observe and record a 15 minute breaktime on a primary school playground as part of a study of children's informal language. This chapter draws on extracts from some of their recording and observation on playgrounds in Bedfordshire, Cambridgeshire, Hertfordshire, Northamptonshire and Milton Keynes. Their data could be grouped under several headings: jokes, traditional rhymes and games, football, media influences and narrative fantasy games. Since the enduring traditional playground games and girls' play, in particular, have been discussed elsewhere (Opie 1993, Bishop and Curtis 2000, Grugeon 2000) it seemed interesting to concentrate on the way recent media influences are being absorbed into the language and culture of the playground.

'Not in front of the grown-ups' – jokes and traditional games

Tracy was not alone when she observed that these games frequently included a forbidden word or two: 'bum', 'knickers', 'arse'. This was particularly the case with games which included songs and rhymes. She wondered whether this could be the reason:

> why these games have a stage on the playground and not in the classroom or home, or not at least when teacher or mum can hear...Adults do not always appreciate the subversiveness of these songs; they have grown up and forgotten them and the plea-

sure and excitement of singing them. Children enjoy being caught singing these songs, just as a reminder to those adults within earshot that they understand and are capable of understanding more about life than adults think they do.

(Tracy Lee, Luton school, 2000)

As David Crystal says, 'Being naughty with language seems innately attractive' (Crystal 1998, p. 169). In his book *Language Play* he is dismayed that so little attention is paid to children's informal language, believing that 'language play...is a prerequisite for successful reading and spelling' (Crystal 1998, p. 181).

Many students noticed how children in the playground loved to tell jokes: 'Verbal jokes can often reflect children's linguistic understandings and agility more accurately than grammar exercises' (Tann 1991, p. 22). Kate, who had collected a number, remarked, 'most of these were not even remotely amusing', yet it was evident that the children were using puns, alliteration and word order to create humorous effects, 'How does a cow go up the A1? On the mooterway' (Kate Alliston, March 2000). Other students observed and remarked on gender differences; girls often playing games which involved verbal interaction in small, cohesive groups, while boys tended to take up more space with games involving running and chasing: football, Power Rangers and stylised fighting routines. Students were surprised to discover how much language was involved in these very active games.

Football

'Come on, pass it here. Here, here! Do it like this ... Pass it to me. NO, NO, NO! YEP here!' (Kulbir Bansal, large multi-ethnic urban lower school, March 2000).

On a large urban middle school playground, Tom observed that the Year 5 and 6 boys:

virtually all played football throughout their playtime. During the game most of the talk could be split into two categories which were either instruction, like 'kick the ball' or criticism, 'why do you always shoot, can't you pass the ball for a change?' Both categories of interaction involved short sentences and even shorter responses. The four boys who talked most, held high status positions within the group and were all good footballers. They adopted the role of unofficial captains and vice-captains between them. They had the football skills to dominate the game which made it easier for them to dominate the other boys who lacked their confidence.

(Tom Bush, March 2000)

Lara also watched a group of Year 6 boys, in a large junior school on the outskirts of a town, who were also dominating the playground space. She observed that:

the verbal communication on the pitch was loud. The boys shouted short comments to each other. ... However, the game also required the involvement of cooperative skills in order to function effectively.

Like Tom, she noticed that 'certain boys tended to give commands concerning players' position on the pitch, most of which were accepted' and that 'The rules governing who played where ... were obviously clear to the pupils' (Blatchford 1998, p. 69). When she talked to the boys afterwards she found that they were articulate and knowledgeable and that their talk was characterised by a humorous sparring repartee. They also had an impressive knowledge about the game and the linguistic conventions of the football commentator.

S: Rivaldo

B: What Rinaldo?

S: No, Rivaldo, you ponce

B: I say Rinaldo, he's right quick with his feet and pings the ball

G: I say Carno

J: Gininio, or Zola, 'And he's taking the ball down the field, and he's tackled, will he make it ... yes, he scores. It's a goal!'

(Lara Smith, March 2000)

For boys, it was evidently important to be 'hard' and good at football. It was one of the ways in which they were negotiating their masculine identity. At the same time, the girls were excluded and marginalised by these games.

Girls on the edge

Many students explored gender issues. Louise was interested by a game called 'Go-Gos' which was played by both boys and girls in Year 5 in her rural middle school.

> The game involves all players placing a Go-Go (a small plastic figure) on the floor in front of a wall. Players take it in turns to throw another Go-Go to try and knock one over ... the game is very popular with both boys and girls, but is always played in single sex groups.   (Louise Bundy, March 2000)

A girl explained, 'We don't play with boys 'cos they're better at, erm ... throwing and stuff, aren't they?' And Louise noted that the boys 'bagsied' the best positions for playing Go-Gos, 'leaving the girls to play in areas where interruptions were more likely'. The boys' confident behaviour in the playground was reflected in their language; girls were more passive in their conversations with her, while the boys tended to interrupt and speak over each other. She also noted that football, played only by boys:

> involves the use of exclusive language with expressions such as 'down the line' and other specialist vocabulary ... vernacular language, including swearing was also evident. ... The boys often play football in role and 'become' Michael Owen or Alan Shearer, changing to Tony Adams or Sol Campbell if they are defending. This sometimes follows current 'real life' events. On one occasion, one boy scored a goal and claimed to be Robbie Fowler. He was then informed that it couldn't have been Fowler because he was injured.   (Louise Bundy, March 2000)

Examples from many of the students showed that the media was exerting a powerful influence on children's play; they noted ways in which this emerged in role play games when television 'brings new words into the language' (Keaney and Lucas 1994, p. 43).

'We wanted to play Pokemon'

> 'We wanted to play Pokemon, but we're not allowed the cards anymore so we have to pretend.'   (Year 3 boy)

Spring 2000 was the height of the Pokemon controversy. All students encountered disgruntled groups of children who were no longer allowed to bring their cards to school. Jane, in a Hertfordshire junior school on the outskirts of a large town, asked two Year 4 boys about Pokemon. They explained how they manage without cards:

Child A: Well there's the cartoon you can watch, there are the cards ... but we're not
            allowed them any more.
Jane: Tell me more about the cards then.
Child B: You collect them and play games with them. You try and beat each other
            ... with the powers on the card. On the cards are different Pokemon like
            Picachu, Beedrill and Bulbasaur. If they have more power than the other
            Pokemon they take away the power and can kill them if they want.
Jane: So what are you playing in the playground then?
Child A: Our Pokemon game. He's a Squirtle and he can squirt water, I'm a Beedrill
            and I can drill through things.
Child B: What about the ball?
Child A: Oh yeah, the Power Ball, you can throw at people and make them slow
            down so you use your powers on them.

                                                            (Jane Kisby, March 2000)

On the playground of a large urban multi-ethnic infant school, Anne's interview with
Year 2 boys also explains how children are coping with the Pokemon phenomenon in
the face of disapproval by the adult world. Wherever the cards are banned the children
seem to compensate by absorbing the language and conventions of Pokemon in their
imaginative play.

Anne: What are you going to play?
Child A: Well, we're thinking about playing a game of Pokemon, 'cos we all like
            Pokemon ... I made up Pokemon!
(There is much discussion about the different characters.)
Anne: What normally happens when you play then?
Child A: We make up a Pokemon, then that Pokemon will rescue [indistinct] then
            someone has to be Ash and someone has to be like Team Rocket ...
Anne: Is Ash the leader of the people, the children ...?
Child A: Er, no Ash is the leader of all the Pokemons ...
Anne: So what sort of adventures do you have when you're the Pokemon?
Child A: Um, well we don't normally have *adventures*. Er, Ash goes off with all his
            Pokemons and then he normally comes back with the, er ... medals, and
            does stuff like that ... and my made-up Pokemon was Bulbasaur's umbrella
            and what I need to do is to get my arms in here ... like Bulbasaur's got
            them on his back ... he's got guns that come out of his back but my made-
            up Pokemon ... he's got guns instead of hands.

                                                (Year 2 boys. Anne Lees, March 2000)

Many students recorded similar instances of children absorbing and adapting the
Pokemon characters and stories into their fantasy play. This involved a confident use of
the language of the Pokemon universe.

Swapping and bartering

Jonathan recorded two Year 6 boys actually swapping cards at an urban middle school:

The swapping process uses a varied amount of bartering ... they take strengths of the
Pokemon very seriously as they negotiate fiercely.

Child A: I'm not giving you that for only one Squirtle. It's not worth it. He's only
            got three power points to Charmander's five. No way, nah ... what else?

Child B: That's stupid, 'cos Rychu can have up to seven blast power points if you put him with Squirtle ... yeah?

Child A: No way, it takes too long for them to evolve ... I'm not giving that.

These older boys have a good grasp of the linguistic conventions of bartering. The game itself requires knowledge of both the rules and the strengths and weakness of the characters. Listening to children playing, Jonathan remarked:

The children's skill is highlighted, in particular, when the creatures 'evolve'. This involves two creatures joining as one to become another creature with combined powers. This is, of course, the initial idea of Pokemon, as the name itself is a joining of 'pocket monster'. (Jonathan Smith, March 2000)

The game was intended for children of ten years and over but has swept through the primary sector. In a rural village school, Sarah-Jane recorded two boys during 'wet play' playing with Pokemon cards. Although M is five years old and T is six, they are adept at using the terminology, though not sure of the rules. This is an extract from a much longer transcript.

M: Choose which Pokemon you want to fight with against my Magikarp.

T: Mmm ... [flicking through his cards]. Tangela. Nothing can beat Tangela. He's got loads of health [pointing at the hit points indicated by an HP on the card].

M: Yeah, but choose one that's as good as mine this time. ... Now, which one is your best?

T: Tangela. He can beat anyone.

(Sarah-Jane Simmons, March 2000)

Sarah-Jane comments, 'This card game involves, "... a complicated system of trumps, hit points, attacks and retreats ..." [Neumark 2000]. It is clear from the transcript that neither boy was sure how to play the game correctly and so they had developed their own rules.' On the playground they played a chasing game based on Pokemon, where they took on a role and acted out a narrative based on confrontation between the characters.

As the children's narrative game based on Pokemon was not a traditional game with established rules it incorporated not only a discussion about rules but an attempt on the children's part to make up their own rules [Moyles 1994, p. 7]. This involved a discussion which required them to explain the reasons behind certain rules. For example, one boy aged six, decided there should be somewhere you could go when you 'retreat' in order to show that you were 'retreating' and also because it would enable children to rest if they were tired without fear of being 'attacked'. (Sarah-Jane Simmons, March 2000)

Sarah-Jane felt that there was an element of subversion in this game, 'the very language of Pokemon is subversive, taking ordinary English words and changing them slightly or mixing them together, like, 'Drowzee' and 'Meowth'. Pokemon was not liked by the teaching staff but on the playground the children were more free to do what they wanted, 'Outside the school building lies an area in which the writ of adults play a less decisive part' (Moyles 1994, p. 49).

Clare, in a large village school outside the town of Huntingdon, was also working with Key Stage 1 children. She observed that while the girls were largely engaged in skipping and clapping games:

The boys' entrance to the playground was very different. ... After a couple of loops round the playground they tended to come to a standstill in small groups and take out their Pokemon cards for swaps and battles. Pokemons have become the newest media products to take over the primary school playground; it appears that many children are either playing with their cards or pretending to be Pokemons. This is an example of the huge influence that the media appears to exert over children as young as five. Alongside the Pokemon cards and other merchandise, there is a Pokemon cartoon on television and a Pokemon film has been released in the cinema.

(Clare Drake, March 2000)

Clare felt that this influx of cartoon related products was not a bad thing; through watching television, often alongside their play, children were developing specific skills [Simatos and Spencer 1992, p. 115].

There was one child who was obviously very knowledgeable about Pokemon and how the battles were decided. This meant that he appeared to take on the role of adjudicator and dominate in this way, with many of the children approaching him to clear up disputes they had over who had won the battle and arguments about 'fair swaps'. He is a child who is quiet in the classroom; often refraining from raising his hand because he lacks confidence in his own ability. When I questioned him about the role he appeared to undertake in the playground, he told me that people came to ask him because, 'I've got the most Pokemons and I understand them best'. This showed me that when dealing with a subject he is confident with, he is more than able to express himself clearly to others.   (Clare Drake, March 2000)

Girls can be Pokemonsters

Clare recorded girls participating in Pokemon games, 'either with each other or with boys' and she reflected, 'I think this may be to do with the fact that Pokemon games are played statically and do not involve a high level of aggression or competitiveness'.
Natalie also recorded Year 3 boys and girls playing together.

Child B (boy): This is an energy card, it shows the energy you need to find ...
Child C (girl): She needs fire energy and that means she can flame kick more when she's got energy.
Child B: That one's my favourite card, that's Charmanda.
Child C: Mine's Nine Tails, she's called that because she's got nine tails, look ...

It would seem that the phonological and nonsense features of the language are also part of the fascination of this game. The children engage in a kind of poetic incantation as they are negotiating.

Child A (boy): I've got two Squirtles.
Child B: Squirtle for Beedrill.
Child C: They're the same sort of cards.
Child B: It's not really worth it.
Child C: Can I have Diglett?
Child A: Onix, Charmander, Charizard, Charmeleon, Archemite.
Child C: Don't want Squirtle ! Don't want him!
Child A: Articuno?
Child C: Umm, Arcanine?
Child A: OK.
Child C: No, 'cause he's better. OK have Arcanine.

Child A: Thanks.
Child C: That's OK.

(Natalie Hunter, March 2000)

Other media influences

The Pokemon games reflect the latest media craze but there was much evidence of other media influences. Claire, in a small village school observed six Year 1 children, four boys and two girls, playing a game of what she thought was the traditional chasing game 'It':

Claire: What do you call this game?
Child A: Croc.
Claire: Who taught you to play this game?
Child A: I don't know. I've got Croc on my Playstation.

(Claire Pearson, March 2000)

On a multi-ethnic, urban infant school playground:

> WWF (World Wrestling Federation) was a particularly popular game, during which a child's head was held in an arm-lock, or there was an attempt to pull the child to the ground. Other favourites were Power Rangers. It was apparent that the boys were attempting to imitate the macho images they have seen on the screen.

(Sharon Gooding, March 2000)

Schools on the whole disapprove of wrestling and fighting games but many students observed that children knew the difference between play fights and the real thing and that the former were often quite controlled and stylised performances. Five Year 4 boys demonstrated this as they discussed how they were going to re-enact scenes from WWF.

> The boys would come up with ideas only to have them challenged and discarded by others. There were numerous interruptions when someone was desperate to have their idea heard and sometimes another member of the group would carry these ideas forward. I noticed that the boys would help each other with the technical vocabulary such as the names of wrestlers and their trademark wrestling moves. ... The names and trademark moves of the wrestlers provided a focus for the discussion. Many of the wrestlers have alliterative names, such as 'Scotty Too Hotty' and 'Big Boss Man'. The boys took great delight in shouting these out in the style of the wrestler. The alliterative names seemed to give them immense pleasure and they would be repeated over and over again. ... This led to a member of the group suggesting that they should make up their own names and trademark moves. One pupil invented the name 'Stinkin' Steven' and the trademark move 'Stinkin' Steven Slammer'.

(Clare Fawcett, March 2000)

One of the group then proceeded to tell what had happened on the programme the night before; the group were fascinated and did not speak until he had finished. Clare commented, 'During lesson time pupil A would seldom volunteer an answer but in this case he was very animated and chose his words carefully so as to maintain the attention of the audience'. Clare pondered the importance of teachers being aware of children's culture and the power of storytelling.

Bringing the playground into the classroom?

What implications does this evidence of children's spontaneous informal language outside the classroom offer to teachers of literacy? The students who contributed to this discussion had discovered a rich source of language in the rhymes, jokes and narrative of the playground. They had demonstrated that children's traditional games are alive and well at the start of the twenty-first century and that newer influences were continuing to be absorbed and creatively subverted as they always have been; Popeye the Sailor Man and Pokemon, Shirley Temple and the Spice Girls comfortably co-exist. The student teachers' assignment was to analyse the evidence they had collected and discuss ways in which it would influence their work in the classroom. But that is material for another chapter!

References

Bishop, J. and Curtis, M. (eds) (2000) *Play today in the primary school playground: Life, learning and creativity.* Buckingham: The Open University Press.

Blatchford, P. (1998) *Social life in school – pupils' experience of breaktime and recess from 7–16 years.* London: Falmer Press.

Crystal, D. (1998) *Language Play.* London: Penguin.

Grugeon, E. (2000) 'Girls' playground language and lore. What sort of texts are these?', in Bearne, E. and Watson, V. (eds) *Where texts and children meet,* 98–112. London: Routledge.

Keaney, B. and Lucas, B. (1994) *Looking at language.* Cambridge: Cambridge University Press.

Moyles, J. (1994) (ed.) *The Excellence of Play.* Buckingham: The Open University Press.

Neumark, V. (2000) *TES Primary Magazine,* Spring.

Opie, I. (1993) *The People in the Playground.* Oxford: Oxford University Press.

Opie, I. and Opie, P. (1959) *The Lore and Language of Schoolchildren.* Oxford: Oxford University Press.

Simatos, A. and Spencer, K. (1992) *Children and Media.* Liverpool: Manutius Press.

Tann, S. (1991) *Developing Language in the Primary Classroom.* London: Cassell.

Widdowson, J. (2000) 'Childlore: Gateway to language skills', in Bishop, J. and Curtis, M. (eds) *Play today in the primary school playground: Life, learning and creativity.* Buckingham: The Open University Press.

Acknowledgements

I wish to thank to all members of the De Montfort University 1999/2000 Year 3 Primary BEd Language in Education course and my colleagues Beth Smith and Roger Strangwick. Also, particular thanks to: Kate Alliston, Kulbir Bansal, Louise Bundy, Tom Bush, Clare Drake, Clare Fawcett, Sharon Gooding, Natalie Hunter, Jane Kisby, Tracy Lee, Anne Lees, Claire Pearson, Sarah-Jane Simmons, Jonathan Smith and Lara Smith.

Chapter 2

Having your own voice valued
David Skidmore

In this chapter, I present and analyse two examples of classroom discourse between a teacher and a small group of pupils in primary schools. Both transcripts are extracts from discussions which took place during a guided reading session, part of the daily literacy hour introduced by the British government in primary schools from September 1998 (DfEE, 1998). The hour is divided into four periods of fixed duration, during which specified forms of organisation and activity are to be used. For 20 minutes of the hour, the teacher may take an ability group for guided reading, while the rest of the class works independently. It is from discussions during this period that the extracts below are taken. On the basis of some observable contrasts between the two extracts, I raise some questions about what forms of verbal interaction between pupils and teacher might best contribute to the development of the pupils' independent powers of comprehension. As Wells points out, collaborative talk about texts is an indispensable part of the child's induction into the literate behaviour of their culture (Wells and Chang-Wells 1992).

The discussions were recorded as part of a coursework assignment by two teachers who were students following a programme of advanced professional study; I was their tutor. The students made the recordings in their own classrooms under naturalistic conditions, and gave permission for me to make use of transcribed extracts in this chapter. I have used pseudonyms to disguise the identity of all the participants. I have used the following conventions in transcribing the sequences (Silverman 1997):

[	simultaneous speech
(Docky)	obscure speech (words inside the parentheses represent the transcriber's best estimate of what is being said)
[...]	omitted speech
(.)	pause of one second or longer
=	'latched' utterances, with no silence between them
No.	bold font indicates speech which is louder than the surrounding discourse (typically, where the speaker is emphasising a point)
° Oh yeah. °	degree symbols surround speech which is lower in volume than the surrounding discourse
'He heard a dog'	single quotation marks surround discourse which represents verbatim reading from the text
(*laughs*)	italics within parentheses indicate contextual information interpolated by the transcriber

Sequence One: True or false?

Sequence One is taken from a discussion involving five Year 5 pupils in a multicultural primary school in south-east England. There is one girl in the group, Fiona, who is identified as having general learning difficulties; the four boys each have statements for specific learning difficulties (one of the boys is silent during the sequence transcribed below). Before this discussion, the pupils had taken turns to read a story called *Rocky's Fox* (Krailing 1998); they are now asked to consider a series of statements about the story and determine whether they are (i) true (ii) false, or (iii) there is not enough evidence to decide. They are familiar with this type of task, though the text is new to them. As we join the discussion, they are considering the statement 'He [i.e. Rocky, the main character] heard a dog barking'; in understanding the sequence it will help the reader to know that, in the story, Rocky hears a barking noise which he knows is *not* made by a dog; later, a neighbour tells him that it was a fox. One pupil (Kevin) has already argued that the statement is false, but Fiona disagrees, saying: 'It's true 'cause he did hear a dog barking.' The teacher re-reads the relevant section of the story with Fiona, then continues:

1. Teacher:		Right. So is it true or false? (Docky) knew the sound (.) erm (.) 'He heard a dog barking.' Did he hear in the first picture on the first page did he hear that barking (.) to be a dog?
2. Fiona:		Yes.
3. Teacher:		It wasn't a dog (.) Fiona.
4. Pupils:		[Fox. [False =
5. Teacher:		= It was false because it was a fox barking. How does he know it was a fox barking? 'Cause he described it to Mr Keeping later on and Mr Keeping said **ha** that's a fox bark. Fox (.) foxes bark like that. Do you understand? Not really do you?
6. Fiona:		Erm. (*Fiona shakes her head*).
7. Teacher:		Why do you think that it's a dog barking? You tell me **one** piece of information from that story to tell you that it's a dog.
8. Fiona:		Because erm foxes don't bark and dogs does (.) do.
9. Alex:		Foxes [do.
10. Teacher:		[OK look at page six Fiona.
11. Alex:		Foxes bark like that.
12. Teacher:		Page six? OK. Read it with me.
13. Teacher and Fiona:		'The next day Rocky saw Mr Keeping. He told him about the noise.'
14. Teacher:		What noise Fiona? What noise?
15. Fiona:		The noise what the fox was making.
16. Teacher:		The noise that the fox was making. Which noise was the fox making?
17. Fiona:		A dog (.) noise. (*Fiona laughs*).
18. Teacher:		He was barking. The fox was barking yeah? So the noise that he heard in the night. So he told him about the noise. Carry on (.) reading (.) page six. 'That' =
19. Teacher and Fiona:		= 'will be a fox said Mr Keeping. Foxes bark like that.'

20. Teacher:	So.
21. Alex:	It's true =
22. Teacher:	= So the noise he heard on that first page was a bark. He thought it **might** have been a dog.
23. Fiona:	It wasn't.
24. Teacher:	But it **wasn't** a dog. What was it?
25. Fiona:	He knew it wasn't a dog.
26. Teacher:	What was it?
27. Fiona:	It was a fox.
28. Teacher:	It was a fox. And the statement says on your sheet 'He heard a dog barking.' Did he hear a dog barking?
29. Kevin:	**No**.
30. Teacher:	So is it true or false?
31. Fiona:	[False.
32. Richard:	[It
	was false.
33. Teacher:	Do you understand?
34. Fiona:	° Yes. °
35. Teacher:	OK next sentence.

The tone and rhythm of the dialogue in this extract largely conforms to the properties of the 'recitation script' which typifies much classroom interaction: according to Gutierrez (1994) the teacher selects pupil speakers; there is little or no acknowledgement of pupil self-selection; pupil responses tend to be short, and the teacher does not encourage elaboration of responses; and the teacher uses many 'test' questions, where the implied role of the pupil is to contribute a predetermined 'right' answer in response. One factor which may contribute to this outcome is the nature of the published support materials which the teacher is using. These materials construct a heavily constrained form of comprehension activity: for each statement about the story which the pupils are asked to discuss, only three possible answers are available (true/false/not enough evidence), and in each case only one of these is deemed 'correct'. Publishers may claim, and teachers be led to believe, that this kind of material is particularly suited to pupils who experience difficulties with reading, on the grounds that it offers a 'structured' approach to the teaching of comprehension skills. My interpretation of this episode, however, suggests that such 'teacher-proof' materials carry a risk of lodging classroom talk into its default groove of recitation, to the detriment of pupils' independent powers of comprehension.

Allowing for the constraints imposed by the support materials in this case, we might nevertheless ask whether alternative responses by the teacher at specific points could have lent a more productive turn to the dialogue. Would Fiona's learning have been better assisted, for example, if at turn 3 the teacher had requested her to elaborate on the reasoning behind her (mistaken) thinking, instead of making a straightforward contradiction? What if Fiona's statement 'foxes don't bark' (turn 8) had been treated as an opportunity to open the floor to other pupils, rather than directing the group's attention immediately back to the text? These instances can be seen as *critical turning-points* in the discourse, where the teacher's utterances influence the shape and tone of the subsequent interaction, in this case pushing it in the familiar direction of teacher-dominated recitation, but where alternative choices were available which might have challenged the pupils to engage in a higher level of literate thinking.

Sequence Two: Who is most to blame?

The second sequence is taken from a discussion among five pupils in a vertically-grouped Year 5/6 class in a multicultural urban primary school in south-east England. The group comprises two girls and three boys; for three of the group English is an additional language; two of the pupils were on the school's register of special educational needs at the time of the recording, one having a statement of special educational needs. The group are discussing their views on the characters in a story called 'Blue Riding Hood' (Hunt 1995), which they have just read together. This is a modern parody of the familiar fairy tale, rewritten to subvert the stereotypical characters and events of the original story. The notes which accompany the story suggest that none of the characters behave very well, but some might be seen as better than others; the pupils are asked to discuss the story and try to put the characters in order, from least to most blameworthy. As we join the discussion, the group has just been talking about the character of the wolf in the story; the teacher now moves them on to consider others.

1. Teacher:	Okay we have other characters. Who should we discuss next?
2. Ian:	Erm (.) the woodcutter.
3. Teacher:	Where does he come on the scale?
4. Ian:	Near the end.
5. Suma:	Because when she was wandering around in the forest and he met her and the he told her that he's going to show her grandmother how to behave (.) and he had an axe and (.) the the (.) he took the skin off the wolf and he killed grandma.
6. Ian:	No they didn't know there was bears in the forest and erm there they thought she would just get lost in the woods.
7. Kulvinder:	But the woodcutter bashed granny's door down.
8. Penda:	I don't think he was well behaved (.) because he should have come and talked to her not smash her house down.
9. Suma:	Yeah but granny still behaved in the same way even when the woodcutter was in her house.
10. Kulvinder:	Granny (.) was mean and she was just horrible she just tells her to get out of the house. [...] (*There is a hiatus in the transcript at this point because the audiotape had to be changed while the group continued to talk.*)
11. Teacher:	Okay should we now try to put the characters in some sort of order?
12. Kulvinder:	Woodcutter (.) granny Blue Red Riding Hood and the wolf.
13. Colin:	I had the wolf then the woodcutter then Blue Riding Hood then granny.
14. Ian:	I had Blue Riding Hood the wolf the woodcutter then **granny**.
15. Suma:	The woodcutter the Red Riding Hood the wolf then granny granny.
16. Penda:	The wolf the woodcutter Blue Riding Hood then granny.
17. Teacher:	It is very difficult isn't it? I would say the wolf although we agreed his behaviour was far from perfect. Then I would say (.) you need to think about what happened. Granny threw Blue Riding Hood out of the house yeah? Erm now that was quite deliberate =
18. Ian:	= A **witch**.
19. Penda:	Yeah she started everything it was all her fault (.) if she hadn't thrown Red I mean Blue Riding Hood none of this would have happened.
20. Kulvinder:	But Blue Red Riding Hood killed the wolf.
21. Penda:	° Oh yeah. °

22. Colin:	None of them were really nice.
23. Ian:	No.
24. Penda:	But whose fault was it?
25. Suma:	I think granny's.
26. Colin:	But she didn't kill any one.
27. Penda:	No but it was her fault really wasn't it?
28. Kulvinder:	She wasn't very nice (.) well I didn't like (.) she **deserved** to be eaten.
29. Colin:	She wasn't killed on purpose was she?
30. Ian:	The woodcutter killed her.
31. Colin:	No she was eaten by bears.
32. Ian:	I mean it was his fault he erm chucked her out.
33. Teacher:	Well we have run out of time. I think you have done very well. I thought it was hard to sort them out but you together all of you have done that really well. I don't think there is a right or wrong answer if there was we wouldn't have had much to talk about.

There are several marked contrasts between the discourse in this extract and that in Sequence One, which raise significant questions with regard to efforts to enhance pupils' independent powers of comprehension. It illustrates two important characteristics of the 'responsive-collaborative' script described by Gutierrez (1994). In the first place, there is minimal teacher selection of pupils; pupils self-select, or select other pupils, while the teacher frames and facilitates the activity, but generally adopts a 'light touch' approach to intervention. Secondly, there is 'chaining' of pupil utterances, in which each utterance builds on preceding contributions, qualifying, questioning, or contradicting what previous speakers have said. Whereas in much classroom discourse, the right to ask questions is a privilege reserved to the teacher (Cazden 1988), in this discussion it is normal for pupils to address questions to each other (24, 27, 29). Pupils explain the reasons for their views about the story, challenging and countering each other's thinking; at one point this process seems to lead to a re-evaluation of one element of the story by one of the pupils (turn 21). By pooling their thinking and making it public, they are also encouraged to make it explicit, and to open it up to modification through considering other points of view, with the result that they attain a richer understanding of the story collectively than they would be likely to achieve individually.

A significant contextual difference between Sequence One and Sequence Two is the nature of the comprehension task which the pupils are asked to carry out under the guidance of the teacher. In the present case, the pupils are asked to discuss which character in the story is most to blame, a question to which various answers are possible, none of which is uniquely 'correct'. It is therefore inherent in the nature of the task that they are required to think about the narrative, to retell the story in their own words rather than merely recite it by heart. I would argue that the more open form of discussion which results is better suited than teacher-led recitation to the goal of enhancing pupils' independent powers of comprehension.

In your own words, please!

The conditions under which the two sequences of classroom discourse presented above were produced were sufficiently similar to render a comparison between them of interest from an educational point of view. The size of the groups and the age of the pupils were similar, and both groups were taking part in focused comprehension discussions on the topic of texts which they had just read, during guided reading sessions within the tightly prescribed parameters of the literacy hour. But in spite of these similarities, we have seen that there are significant contrasts between the extracts in the quality of the talk that is produced. I would argue that Sequence One can be seen as an instance of what Bakhtin calls 'pedagogical dialogue', in which 'someone who knows the truth instructs someone who is ignorant of it and in error' (Bakhtin 1984). Sequence Two, on the other hand, resembles Bakhtin's concept of 'internally persuasive discourse', in which pupils are invited to retell the story in their own words (Bakhtin 1984).

An important question raised by my analysis is the appropriateness of comprehension exercises based on a forced-choice task structure where the text in question is a literary one. In both sequences, the teacher and pupils were discussing texts belonging to the genre of short narrative fiction. However, in Sequence One, their responses were constrained by the requirement to respond to propositional statements about the text, and to assign them to one of a fixed range of categories (true/false/not enough evidence). This seems far from an authentic model of the kinds of process in which experienced readers engage when reading and evaluating literary texts, such as fictional narratives; indeed, it is difficult to think of any situation outside the classroom where readers would need to respond to a literary text like this. I would suggest that the critical understanding and appreciation of literary texts is a cultural practice which can, and should, be deliberately taught in schools, but that crucially it needs to be seen as a *non-algorithmic* form of knowledge. If we reduce pupils' experience of this branch of literacy to the recitation of 'facts' about a story, then we are not presenting them with a simplified version of the task to be mastered; we are misrepresenting the nature of that task. This does not imply that teachers should not attempt to structure their pupils' encounters with literary texts, but rather that there are other, more open-ended kinds of question or activity (such as the example in Sequence Two) which can be used to focus their discussion or writing, and which provide pupils with an opportunity to participate actively in shaping their own understanding of and orientation towards the text. One could also take this argument further and suggest that, where the aim is to enhance pupils' ability to engage in 'literate thinking' (Wells and Chang-Wells 1992), then *the process is the product*; from this point of view, instead of relying on scores attained in standardised tests, it would be appropriate to base the assessment of pupils' literacy development, at least in part, on an examination of the communicative competence they display in structured group discussions about texts which they have read.

References

Bakhtin, M. M. (1984) *Problems of Dostoevsky's Poetics*, ed. and trans. Emerson, C. Manchester: Manchester University Press.
Cazden, C. B. (1988) *Classroom Discourse: The Language of Teaching and Learning*. Portsmouth, NH: Heinemann.
DfEE (1998) *The National Literacy Strategy: Framework for Teaching*. London: DfEE.
Gutierrez, K. D. (1994) 'How talk, context, and script shape contexts for learning: a cross-case comparison of journal sharing', *Linguistics and Education* **5**, 335–65.
Hunt, G. (1995) *Reading: Key Stage Two, Scottish Levels C-E*. Leamington Spa: Scholastic.
Krailing, T. (1998) *Rocky's Fox*. Walton-on-Thames: Nelson.
Silverman, D. (ed.) (1997) *Qualitative Research: Theory, Method and Practice*. London: Sage.
Wells, G. and Chang-Wells, G. L. (1992) *Constructing Knowledge Together: Classrooms as Centers of Inquiry and Literacy*. Portsmouth, NH: Heinemann.

Chapter 3

Circle Time
Carol Smith

Picture the end of another desperate day; distraught over my cup of tea. Paul, new to the class, had let me know how he felt about me. He was certainly articulate:

'You hate me, you f...ing fat bitch.'
'You bloody hate me, you big ugly cow.'

And so it had gone on. Paul was a child 'beyond himself' and I was beyond coping with him. The rest of my poor Year 4 class were falling apart too, victims of Paul's anger, frustration and violent temper. He had been in my class for a week, at the beginning of the summer term, and had well and truly upset the positive atmosphere the class had established.

The incident described above happened twelve years ago and marked when I first came to use Circle Time. Soon after this moment of crisis I was helped by a wonderful teacher, Peter Sadler, from the local Behaviour Support Team. He came to work with me in the classroom alongside Paul, with his extreme emotional and behavioral difficulties. Peter modelled Circle Time for me and, once it became established in the classroom, the effect was magical. It helped the class understand and come to terms with Paul's difficulties and it gave Paul a safe environment in which he felt valued and respected. It took time though. And I had a lot to learn.

Over a period of six weeks with almost daily Circle Times we slowly put our class back together. In a video of Circle Time made at the end of the summer term, no one would be able to single Paul out as the troubled child he had been on arrival. He still spent part of each day under the table or behind the curtains but, through the daily use of Circle Time, the situation gradually improved for everyone. Paul began to talk in an acceptable way and the other children listened and gave him constructive advice on how to modify his behaviour. The experience proved to be major turning points in Paul's attitude and in my classroom management.

The most significant change was the introduction regular of Circle Time. I found that I was not alone in solving Paul's problem. The whole class became involved. Circle Time allowed me to use the children's influence to help reform Paul's behaviour. We never mentioned Paul by name but by using sentence starters such as: 'When someone in our class swears at me it makes me feel...' and 'When a child in our class refuses to come to assembly it makes me feel...'.

Paul gradually became aware of the effect he was having on the class. Without ever naming him, the children could offer suggestions to help him.

'Instead of swearing, it is better to...'
'When I'm angry I...'
'I feel like hiding when...'

Paul's case was extreme but not unique. Circle Time can have a powerful effect on a child's inappropriate behaviour when it is discussed without direct naming or shaming. For the child whose behaviour is under discussion it can be painful. Even without names being mentioned they can usually identify themselves but the pain can be private and the resulting effect is far greater than any achieved through one-to-one adult and child discussions. Of course, teachers need to handle such situations very sensitively and ensure that positive comments and supportive advice are followed through.

After the initial introduction to Circle Time, I attended workshops and seminars led by Jenny Mosley who is now a freelance consultant and writer about Circle Time. Her books *Turn Your School Round* (1993) and *Quality Circle Time* (1996) are valuable reading for anyone interested in trying this strategy for themselves. Over the years since Peter's help, I have consistently found that Circle Time makes a well-behaved class even better and makes a challenging class more manageable. However, Circle Time is not purely about behavioral management. Along with improved behaviour comes the benefits of better speaking and listening skills leading to a more articulate classroom and thus better learning across the curriculum. In this chapter, with reference to my own classroom situation, I will describe the purposes and organisation of Circle Time.

How does Circle Time work?

For some children in school it can be difficult to say things and to have them heard! Circle Time provides an oasis of calm in a packed timetable when everyone has equal responsibility and opportunity to speak and listen in a group they can trust. The secure situation promotes confident speech. There is a space where children can feel confident and comfortable when expressing their opinions, explaining their learning or discussing their ideas. A forum for the honest expression of emotions and feelings within a secure structure is perhaps the most beneficial aspect of Circle Time.

Circle time is underpinned by a number of simple principles.

- Everyone in the class sits in a circle. On its own, sitting in a circle gives everyone equal status and an equal voice. There is no hierarchy. Everyone has a right to speak and to be heard. To emphasise this a 'talking object' is used, such as a stone or toy – children may only speak when holding the 'talking object'.
- Everyone has a chance to speak. No child should be interrupted when speaking, emphasising the need to listen with mutual and growing respect.
- No child is ever forced to speak; there is no pressure to contribute. If they do not want to comment children simply pass the 'talking object' when it reaches them. Silence is respected.
- Names of children in the circle are never mentioned unless it is to say something good about them. The atmosphere of Circle Time is always positive about the children and when difficult issues are discussed it is always in a constructive way.
- Anything discussed in the circle remains confidential.

Circle Time has set rituals and formalities to fit with these principles which set it apart from other lessons. Everyone sits in the circle at the same level either on chairs or on the carpet. The only exceptions to this in my classroom are for children with injuries or 'the special person of the week' who always sits in the rocking chair. This is a special chair in the class, where I normally sit for registration, shared reading and writing times and mental maths sessions in the numeracy hour, and where sick or sad children sit if they need comfort. It is a very old chair but has bright, comfortable cushions. I never sit in it for Circle Time.

In my classroom, the basic structure of the 30 minutes has stayed the same since I first began using Circle Time as a regular feature of my practice. However, different classes can have different rituals and rules and these may be adapted over time. Some classes like to remove their shoes, some shut themselves off from the rest of the school, some like to move to a quieter place, others prefer to re-arrange the furniture in their own room. All classes should have a 'talking object' which you have to be holding in order to speak. Guests visiting the classroom should be expected to sit in the circle too. No one is allowed to sit outside, not even OFSTED Inspectors (yes, in my class he put his clipboard down and joined in!). The 'talking objects' can be ceremoniously placed in the middle of the circle for guests or 'special people' to choose. Once everyone is comfortable and the talking object in place, Circle Time is ready to begin.

Figure 3.1

Time and space

Circle Time needs to be regular and valued. In my class it was seldom cancelled – the children wouldn't let me! It is important to set time aside in your timetable. You also need to plan where you will do it. In my school the classroom was often the only option so I put up with five minutes of table moving at the beginning and end of the Circle Time to create the appropriate environment. In fact, this became a useful preparation time for me and the children, enabling us to switch in to a Circle Time mood.

What do we talk about?

Opening words

In Circle Time the spotlight moves away from individual children quickly so that no one either monopolises the talk or feels under pressure to say something if they do not want to. Some children only speak quietly but have the right to be listened to as intently as the louder children. Sentence openers, or talking frames, help children who are shy or anxious about speaking in front of the whole class by giving them the security of having a contribution started for them. As the talking object is passed around the circle, each child repeats an opening statement; for example, 'Something I really enjoy at the weekend is …' or 'It makes me sad when …' While they wait for their turn children can clarify their thoughts and prepare their finishing phrases. Some will repeat the words of others or, alternatively, they can pass and no one will think any less of them. Sometimes quiet children remain reticent for many weeks but I have never taught a class where children refused to join in every week. In my classroom, if a child is finding it difficult to contribute, I will try to sit next to them until they feel secure enough to speak. Talking frames also help those children who have so much to say that they lose their way when talking and forget the focus of their contribution. It is important to keep the discussion focused and clear. When they become experienced with Circle Time, children can formulate their own talking frames as sentence starters to structure their talk. They can plan their suggestions and 'post' them on a board in the classroom or put them in a suggestion box. Like writing frames, which become most effective when they can be gradually removed, the talking frames used in Circle Time can be adapted or taken away completely according to the needs of the children.

Taking responsibility

Some of the most important talks we have had in Circle Time have been about behaviour and how to act appropriately in different situations. The children take responsibility for any changes in behaviour that are needed. They learn how to deal with calling out, fighting in the playground or swearing on the football field. The strength of decisions made in Circle Time comes from the discipline and control being shared rather than being imposed by an adult. There is a sense of collective responsibility.

Improving self-esteem

Circle Time has a great effect on children's self-esteem. This works not just by children having their opinions listened to and valued, but by regular opportunities to be the 'special' person. During this time at the beginning of a Circle Time session a child can hear thirty or more reasons why people like them.

> 'I like Sarah because she helps me with my maths.'
> 'I like Jordan because he is always smiling.'
> 'I like Simone because she's good at football'.

This is the one time when children cannot pass! The children being talked about always say at the end that it felt embarrassing but that it was good to hear positive things said about them.

What about difficult issues being mentioned?

Difficult things will be brought up in Circle Time but I've found that children will only tell what they want everyone to know. For example, it took Melanie until the summer term before she told us that 'Something she needed help with was …' that her father had left the family at Christmas to go 'on business in Singapore' and the only communication they had received from him was a postcard to say he was not coming back. The silence following Melanie's announcement was deafening. As the talking object (on this occasion a teddy) went around the circle the children came up with a range of suggestions to help her:

'Put an advert in the paper'
'Ask the Salvation Army'
'Write to the Prime Minister'
'Get a private detective'.

I have found that it is a relief for children when they can tell, rather than hide, worrying things about themselves. No child has ever revealed something in the circle that I felt should not be kept just in the circle

Emergency Circle Time

When there are crises in the class (usually immediately after a fight on the playground or similar), Circle Time is an effective way to deal with them. The main reason for this is that it slows down response, allowing you time to find out the full facts and giving the children the chance to have a say before any action is taken. Often during an emergency Circle Time I say nothing at all. Apologies are made, hands are shaken and everyone is able to get on with their work after a few minutes. A major crisis is caused if someone breaks one of the rules of Circle Time, such as gossiping in the playground about what has been said. This sort of problem may take longer to resolve.

Circle Time and the National Curriculum

The programme of study for speaking and listening in the National Curriculum for English (DfEE and QCA 1999) requires children to:

- speak with confidence;
- listen, understand and respond appropriately;
- talk effectively as members of a group.

The National Literacy Strategy *Framework for Teaching* (DfEE 1998), from Year 1 Term 1 to Year 6 Term 3 requires children to be taught oral skills as varied as how to; retell stories, discuss, recite, comment on, read aloud, discriminate orally, identify and discuss, pose questions, evaluate, read and present, rehearse and improve, summarise orally, collaborate, present a point of view, explain, articulate personal responses and finally, contribute constructively to shared discussion about literature, responding to and building on the views of others. What a powerful classroom, with so many 'articulate' verbs at work! It is our job as teachers to give our children the tools to take part in such a rich talking and learning environment. They need the self-confidence to take a full and active part in shared reading and writing sessions and plenary sessions, where they are being asked to discuss key issues in their work. Circle Time is the ideal structured and safe classroom situation to help teachers achieve this as well as to improve speaking and listening skills.

Improvement in speaking and listening made through Circle Time is incidental and not the main learning objective. However, articulate talk is caught rather than deliberately taught and all of the aspects of speaking and listening listed above are enhanced by Circle Time. This is particularly so through the modelling of purposeful talk by the class teacher, any other adults present and fluent children. Less confident children have the chance to try out talk in a supportive atmosphere. As speaking and listening skills develop, the models provided by more confident speakers provide a scaffold to assist children's performance. Circle Time also allows for any weakness in speaking because listeners' attention is focused on something other than the performance of each speaker. Listeners concentrate on the meaning of what is being said, not on how it is being presented. If there are poor listeners you may have to work hard for some time to encourage better listening. Circle Time will not give its benefits without effort. Persist and, if you believe in it, it will succeed. Good learning behaviours will follow.

Through realising that their views are valued and appreciated in Circle Time the children's confidence and enthusiasm for talking in other curriculum contexts is increased and better organised. Children do become better listeners, with calling out and interrupting replaced by turn taking and patient attention to the views of others. Children feel safer to contribute to all types of curriculum discussion, they come to view things differently, appreciating new ideas and realising more fully the extent of their own understanding.

Getting started

If you have not used Circle Time before you might prefer to try simple activities at first. Start by re-arranging the furniture and just reading or singing in the circle. Next try a warm-up game like 'Fruit Salad'. This is a game where each child in turn round the circle is named after a fruit, e.g. apple, pear, banana, grape – apple, pear, banana, grape. The teacher (also a fruit!) asks all the apples to change places – then all the pears, all the bananas and so on until everyone has changed places. Finally she says 'Fruit Salad' and everyone swaps places at the same time. Great fun! It also gives an opportunity to manipulate where you sit.

After a warm-up activity you might be ready to try a simple talking frame such as:

'I am really good at ...'
'On Saturdays I really like to ...'
'If I could be a bird I would like to be ...'

And for the 'special person of the week':

'I like Sarah because ...'

Introduce the talking object which gives each person the opportunity to speak. Take time and allow the children to pass if they want to.

Once you feel more confident you can introduce more open, thought-provoking talking frames which encourage more considered responses from the children. For example:

'I feel upset when...'
'If I was Prime Minister for the day I would ...'

However, it is always wise to finish on a lighter note:

'I am really looking forward to ...'
'The first thing I will do on the playground is ...'
'The first thing I will do when I get home is ...'

You could then try an 'Electric Squeeze' to finish. Everyone holds hands (there may be some reluctance at first) and the teacher 'turns on' the electricity by squeezing the hand of the child next to her. That child then passes it to the next child and so on round the circle until it comes back to the teacher. This game encourages everyone to be gentle and helps concentration. Some children like to close their eyes so they do not see the squeeze coming. It is a quiet and calming way to round off the session.

Figure 3.2

Circle Time from the children's point of view

Children in Year 6 chose to put a conch shell, their Circle Time talking object, into a time capsule which was to be buried in the school grounds in January 2000 as part of celebrations for a new millennium. It had been a hard decision for the year group. Only one item could be put in the capsule – would it be the Key Stage 2 SATs papers or a talking object? Following the decision, the children wrote a set of instructions to accompany the shell during a shared writing session. Their writing neatly sums up the principles of Circle Time and indicates how they felt about it:

Circle Time is a safe time where you can talk about your worries and problems, find out more about each other, share good ideas and have fun. We would like you to do Circle Time because it is our favourite subject.

★ *Do Circle Time at least once a week for at least twenty minutes.*
★ *Everyone should respect the circle and if they break the 'Golden Rules' they will be asked to stand outside the circle. This is a horrible feeling and no one in our class has broken this rule, ever.*
★ *Anything talked about in the circle stays in the circle and is not gossiped about on the playground.*
★ *Everyone has the right to 'pass' and not talk. You may only speak when you are holding the talking object or in open forum*
★ *Make a circle of children, chairs, teachers, helpers and any visitors.*
★ *Put the 'talking object' (the shell) in the middle of the circle.*
★ *Begin by playing a warm-up game to mix children up, e.g. Fruit Salad, Zoom Zoom Eek, TV Favourites, I have a basket ...*
★ *Pick a person to be 'special' for that week. Everyone must say something good about them. 'I really like Katie, Barry, Aimie, Asif because ...', 'Ian is special to me because ...'*
★ *Choose a light hearted starting phrase such as 'What I've enjoyed most this week is ...', 'If I was a colour I would be ...', 'When I am older I would like to be ...'*
★ *Choose a more serious starting phrase, such as: 'Something I need help with is...', 'My worry about the playground is ...'*
★ *Finish with 'My wish for the basket' or 'What I'm most looking forward to at the weekend/holiday is ...'*
★ *Lastly close Circle Time with the 'Electric Squeeze'. (You must find out what that is yourselves!)*
★ *Choose some more talking objects as well as the shell. We have one or two teddies, an interesting stick, a model of a 'Talking Head' and a little wooden cat.*

We hope you will like doing Circle Time as much as us.
Love from Year 6 1999/2000

Conclusion

In a primary classroom, Circle Time is a unique time in the week set aside to discuss good things that have happened or concerns the children may have about work or behaviour. It is also a forum for the teacher to raise issues they may wish to talk about and discuss. Whether viewed as a means of managing behaviour, the provision of an opportunity to increase self-esteem or a way of covering the requirements of the National Curriculum it should be a regular part of every articulate classroom.

References

DfEE (1998) *National Literacy Strategy Framework for Teaching*. London: DfEE.
DfEE and QCA (1999) *The National Curriculum: Handbook for Primary Teachers in England*. London: DfEE/QCA.
Mosley, J. (1993) *Turn Your School Round*. Wisbech: Learning Development Aids.
Mosley, J. (1996) *Quality Circle Time*. Wisbech: Learning Development Aids.

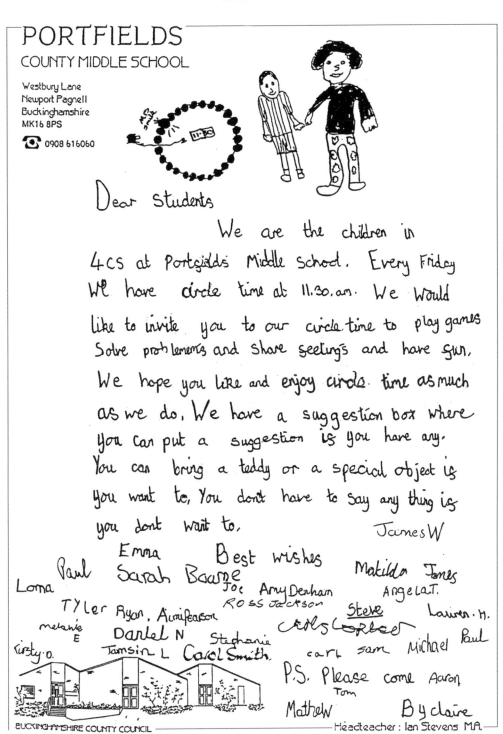

PORTFIELDS

COUNTY MIDDLE SCHOOL

Westbury Lane
Newport Pagnell
Buckinghamshire
MK16 8PS

☎ 0908 616060

Dear Students

We are the children in 4CS at Portfields Middle school. Every Friday we have circle time at 11.30.am. We Would like to invite you to our circle time to play games Solve problements and share feelings and have fun. We hope you like and enjoy circle time as much as we do. We have a suggestion box where you can put a suggestion is you have any. You can bring a teddy or a special object is you want to, You dont have to Say any thing is you dont want to.

Best wishes

P.S. Please come By claire

James W
Emma
Paul
Loma
Sarah Baumte
Joe   Amy Denham
Ross Jackson
Matilda James
Angela T.
TYLer Ryan, Aimee son
melanie
E
Daniel N
kirsty.o.
Tamsin L
Stephanie
Carol Smith.
Steve
Carls Corbce
carl
sam
Michael
Lauren. H.
Paul
Aaron
Tom
Mathew

BUCKINGHAMSHIRE COUNTY COUNCIL ————————— Headteacher: Ian Stevens MA.

Figure 3.3

Chapter 4

Speak for yourself
Prue Goodwin

Has it ever struck you how much we adults talk to ourselves? When I was very young, and prone to chatter away to myself, my older brother regularly pointed out to me that talking to yourself is the first sign of madness. I remember being quite concerned by his warnings and relieved to find no signs of hairs growing on the palms of my hands.[1] But I was no different from any other child who engages in lone 'conversations'. There is evidence that talking to yourself is widespread among the very young, as demonstrated, for example, by the crib monologues observed by Ruth Weir (1962) and Katherine Nelson (1996). Listening to children in the role play area of any nursery or early years classroom, or to the totally absorbed ten-year-old mathematician as she works on a number problem, are experiences common to all primary teachers. Such commentaries on activity are recognised as important aspects of children's growing language competencies. Piaget (1959) described them as egocentric speech. But surely all that 'talking to yourself' disappears as we become more experienced with language and learn to socialise? I am long passed childhood and, the truth is, I still talk to myself on occasions and, listening to other adults, it seems most people do on many occasions. For example, when learning how to print from a computer screen for the first time, I discovered myself saying aloud: 'Into file ... right, what now? ... oh, yes ... come on little arrow ... click on print ... and I need OK ... is that it?' As there is usually no one else present when adults talk to themselves, there must be a reason for these soliloquies that has nothing to do with the need to communicate.

Discounting artificial social events such as swearing at the car or talking to a pet, I notice that I regularly talk aloud to myself for a variety of purposes and I suspect most adults would find the same. The purposes include:

- announcing intentions *I'll have a coffee and then go to the shops.*
- exclamations of annoyance or delight *Look at the state of this room!*
- questions and answers *Who the hell's that?* (on hearing the telephone ring)
- repetition of explanations *Turn left at the lights* (while driving).
- running commentary on activity *Now what have I got to do here? Put screw A into hole B ... come on you devil ... get in there ...* (on constructing DIY furniture)
- articulating a mental activity ... *calculating a sum or listing letters in a spelling.*

Put any of these statements into social situations and they seem perfectly acceptable interactions. Take, for example, a colleague who, at the end of a staff meeting, announces to her assembled friends, 'I'm off to Sainsbury's' – or someone who makes the statement, 'Look at this pile of marking!'. Such declarations would not be described as talking to yourself yet they do not require any verbal response from the listeners. These utterances are

---

[1] The first sign of madness is talking to yourself, the second is hairs growing on the palms of your hands and the third looking for them.

acting as a focus for the speaker's thoughts, in these cases, about their next action. Talking *for* yourself in this way does not only happen while you are alone. But whether with others or alone, there is plenty of evidence to show that when tackling new ideas, such as learning to word-process, articulating the different operations as you go enhances the quality of the learning (Britton 1970, DES 1975, Wells 1987). In fact, the evidence is so overwhelming that talking to learn, and its importance in working on understanding (Barnes 1992), is an aspect of speaking and listening that teachers cannot afford to neglect. In this chapter, I review what major scholars have said on this field of language and learning, using analysis of class-based examples recorded during my observations in schools.

Talking, thinking and learning

Social and cognitive dimensions of talk both play vital roles in the primary classroom. Social talk involves communication between people, interacting with them at a variety of levels according to context. Cognitive talk consists of interaction of ideas – from thought to thought rather than from person to person. It calls on the ability to hypothesise, to make suppositions and to speculate. Cognitive talk is tentative, being exploratory in nature and consequently uncertain in outcome. It is not dependent on the social context but, cognitive talk, and the subsequent learning that takes place, can happen as part of any interaction as well as during those occasions when we talk to ourselves. For specific learning to take place – as in school – a social context may be contrived to encourage the individual learners within a group to articulate their learning (e.g. a seminar in higher education, preschool children at the sand tray or a small group working together in a primary classroom). Take, for example, an extract from the Cumbrian County Council video *Talking sense: oracy group work in the primary classroom* (see References), which demonstrates the two aspects of talk, social and cognitive, in operation. The session involves four children, all under the age of seven, engaged in making individual examinations of the content of owl pellets.

Andrew: I'm digging deep now. I'll bring this giant over ... hey, this is a whopping piece of bone, isn't it? It's a whopping piece.
Emily: I don't think it's a bone Andrew.
Andrew: No ... I'm only joking ... ah ... what is this?
John: I've found a vole jaw.
Emily: I'll see if I can ...
Andrew: What is this? What is this ... is this?
Emily: I've found some fur and it's still dry.
John: It hasn't got any teeth on.
Emily: No.
Sarah: I've got two teeth.
Andrew: Ah ... aha ... a limb ... a limb.
Emily: How do you know it's a limb?
Andrew: 'cause I recognise the shape ... aha ... oho ... aha ... I'm surprised the fur isn't on the outside. Are you surprised ... Emily ... that all the ...? You would have thought that all the fur ... would be on the outside, wouldn't you? But it's not. You found a piece that's still dry ... it's amazing.

Both the cognitive and the social dimensions of talk are clear during this dialogue. There is no doubt that the children are interacting with each other – they give answers to questions and make comments on each other's contributions when required – but there are also times when no response is expected or necessary. Although not ostensibly talking to themselves on such occasions, the children are certainly speaking *for* themselves rather than for any social purpose. In fact, there is a remarkable similarity between the occasions when no response is necessary and the list of instances when adults talk to themselves:

- announcing intentions　　　　　　　　　*I'll bring this giant over*
- exclamations of annoyance or delight　　*Ah ... aha ... a limb ... a limb*
- questions and answers　　　　　　　　　*What is this ... is this?*
- repetition of explanations　　　　　　　*I'm digging deep now ...*
- running commentary on activity　　　　　*I've got two teeth*
- articulating a mental activity　　　　　　*I'll see if I can ...*

Is this a coincidence, or is it just the way we all – young and old – talk to ourselves, both in and out of social situations when involved in cognitive tasks such as remembering, problem solving and learning? Take Andrew's contributions to the 'conversation', for example. He announces I'm digging deep now and in doing so is stating his next action and providing a running commentary on the activity in hand. It requires no response from the other children present. Andrew himself makes no immediate response to Emily's statement about finding dry fur but later his comments show that he has thought through the information she provided and had questioned it in the light of his previous knowledge: 'I'm surprised the fur isn't on the outside. Are you surprised ... Emily ... that all the ...? You would have thought that all the fur ... would be on the outside, wouldn't you? But it's not. You found a piece that's still dry ... it's amazing.' His range of comments may have been similar if he had been engaged on the task alone but the contributions made by his friends enabled him to extend the content of his thinking and therefore what he says to his friends.

> Through improvised talk he can shape his ideas, modify them by listening to others, question, plan, express doubt, difficulty and confusions, experiment with new language and feel free to be tentative and incomplete. It is through talk that he comes nearer to others and with them establishes a social unit in which learning can occur and in which he can shape for public use his private and personal view.
>
> (Barnes *et al.* 1971, p. 162)

As they explore the owl pellets, the social interaction of the Cumbrian children provides them with opportunities to develop on a cognitive level by:

- trying out ideas before accepting or rejecting them;
- expressing feelings of doubt and certainty, disappointment and delight;
- giving each other support through the sharing of experience;
- reflecting on their own and each other's learning.

Their 'conversations' reflect the ways in which we all comment on experiences as they happen but in particular they demonstrate the importance of talk to learning. As the children make remarks, question and comment on their activity they are making the new knowledge their own – transforming it into words that enable them to understand new ideas.

A brief history of talking for oneself

Piaget suggested that egocentric speech is unconnected with social functions and that the learning that takes place comes about as a result of the child's interaction with the concrete world. However, noting the amount of talk that goes on between a group of children at this stage, he commented: 'True, when they are together they seem to talk to each other a great deal more than we do about what they are doing, but for the most part they are only talking to themselves' (Piaget 1959, p. 38). Using rather dismissive expressions, such as, 'True … they seem', and 'but … they are only', Piaget implies that the social context is unimportant. He also suggested that at the age of about seven years the need to 'talk to yourself' in this egocentric manner disappears as children become conscious of their social position and less absorbed in themselves.

Vygotsky proposed a different view of egocentric speech. He saw all speech as primarily social in function, the intellect being developed within social interaction. Where Piaget says that egocentric speech disappears around the age of seven, Vygotsky believes that it changes to 'inner speech' or thought:

> Our experimental results indicate that the function of egocentric speech is similar to that of inner speech. It does not merely accompany the child's activity; it serves mental orientation, conscious understanding; it helps in overcoming difficulties; it is speech for oneself, intimately and usefully connected with the child's thinking. Its fate is very different from that described by Piaget. Egocentric speech develops along a rising, not a declining, curve; it goes through an evolution, not an involution. In the end, it becomes inner speech.   (Vygotsky 1988, p. 228)

Vygotsky described a new area of understanding, just beyond the child's present knowledge, as the 'zone of proximal development'. The conversation between teacher and learners about new ideas support the learners' growing understanding. Teachers speak aloud the thought processes that enable them to understand, thus modelling the stages of thinking for their pupils. Teacher and learners act and talk together until the teacher's support is no longer needed. 'What the child can do in cooperation today he can do alone tomorrow' (Vygotsky 1988, p. 188). Vygotsky questioned the disappearance of egocentric speech, explaining how inner speech became a totally separate and differently organised language function: 'The flow of thought is not accompanied by the simultaneous unfolding of speech. The two processes are not identical, and there is no rigid correspondence between the units of thought and speech' (1988, p. 249). While there may be no 'rigid correspondence', Courtney Cazden (1988, p. 3) argues that the title of Vygotsky's book, *Thought and Language*, lost its true meaning in translation from Russian.

> We are immediately in a difficult area of relationships between thought and language, or 'thinking and speech' as the title of Vygotsky's (1962) book should be translated. The change from thought to thinking and from language to speech is more than a quibble about the correct translation from Russian. The shift in each case is to the more dynamic term: from thought as a product to thinking as a mental activity, and from language as a symbolic system to speech as the use of language in social interaction.
>   (Cazden 1988, p. 3)

Cazden implies that active thinking is dependent on speaking aloud, not just on language used as 'inner speech'. This more active view of thinking and speaking extends the need for talking as you learn beyond the early stages of cognitive development. No matter what the age of the learner, learning is consolidated through the articulation of understanding. However, as talking aloud to yourself in the presence of potential 'listeners' can be embarrassing, learners who are socially aware alter the presentation of their spoken thoughts to accommodate an audience. They address anyone present, making tentative statements, asking questions and inviting response. Such conversations may appear social in purpose, but, as James Britton suggests of children at this stage, they are both social and cognitive at the same time:

> Obviously, a child does not give up social forms of speech when he begins to use 'speech for himself'. The two forms are at first undifferentiated, being early social speech in substance, put to two uses. But as the two become established, modification of the form takes two directions: social speech becomes better communication, while speech for oneself becomes less communicative, more individualised, better able to serve the particular purposes and interests of a particular child.
>
> (Britton 1970, p. 57)

Jerome Bruner describes how teachers provide the social framework – or 'scaffolding' – within which a learner's understanding can grow: 'Once dialogue is made possible by the child now being able to represent linguistically the aspects and elements of the operations he has mastered that he can share with an assisting adult, a powerful discourse device becomes available' (Bruner 1988, p. 94). In scaffolded conversations learners can try out ideas, make mistakes and adapt their thinking by listening to others as they work towards understanding. In the following dialogue between eight-year-old children and their teacher during a class field trip to an old, empty building, the teacher provides a 'scaffold' to learning by prompting the learners to explore new ideas.

Ann:	There's a hole.
Barry:	A chimney! A chimney!
Ann:	No – no it's for escaping.
Rajdeep:	Where's the fire?
Ann:	There isn't one.
Rajdeep:	Then why is there a chimney?
Teacher:	Could the hole have another use?
Barry:	What?
Ann:	There could be a cooker.
Teacher:	If smoke doesn't go out perhaps something comes in.
Rajdeep:	Air comes in.
Barry:	Air! Air! It's a ventilating thing …

The youngsters are prepared to offer ideas that are speculative because the social relationships between teacher and learners are secure. In their speculative remarks, the risk of failure to get the correct answer to the puzzle is a positive challenge to be overcome rather than as a confidence-sapping fullstop to learning. By questioning, stating, arguing and listening to the other members of the group the children's ideas gradually take shape around a piece of knowledge. As Barnes (1992) points out: 'The readiest way of working on understanding is often through talk, because the flexibility of speech makes it easy for us to try out new ways of arranging what we know, and easy to change them if they seem inadequate.'

Talking in class

Talk in primary classrooms involves a range of purposes and, of course, becoming a confident language user in any social situation is of vital importance. However, in planning for speaking and listening, teachers must not neglect the area of cognitive talk. This will require the provision of activities and tasks that require speculation, hypothesis and supposition and which will involve learners in 'talking for themselves' as they discuss the problems they are trying to solve. The aspects of social talk that cater for the needs of listeners – for example, volume or clarity of expression – no longer have as much significance. When talking to learn, the ephemeral nature of talk – with its repetitions, hesitations, unfinished utterances and exaggerated use of fillers (such as ums and ahs) – becomes far more apparent. These characteristics of cognitive talk are illustrated by 'listening' to a group of eight-year-olds working together on a mathematical investigation. In the following example, Katherine, David and Colin discuss how many different ways they can cut an oblong in half. The children have a supply of paper shapes to fold and cut as they wish.

Katherine:	That's not in half ... and that's not in half, is it? It's more like an ice-cube. [laughter]
David:	Go like that and then fold that over like ...
Colin:	That would be a quarter then wouldn't it? Look there ... Yeah but ...
Katherine:	Yeah, but Colin did that way.
Colin:	I've done that way already. We've only got that way. Erm ... er ... um ... I know but you ... and you're allowed to cut it. [teacher walks up] It's very easy this.
Katherine:	Now we've got those two ways. [teacher moves away] Now we've got two ways now haven't we? (to herself) Let's try to get some more ... um ... um ... um ... how many ways? ... if you go like that we ... You can use this paper still. Oh, I've got an idea.
Colin:	I've got an idea.
Katherine:	(to herself) It might not work ... hang on ... just a minute ... it doesn't work ... if that goes across there ... that goes across there ...
David:	Oh yes ... it works.
Katherine:	It works.
Colin:	There you go. Look at that ... there you go. There's one of mine and there's another one of mine.
Katherine:	There's two halves ... two halves ... two halves ... one, two ...
Teacher:	(observing from across the room) Katherine, is that accurate?
Katherine:	No ... no it's not accurate.
David:	Um ... It would be if I'd used a ruler.
Katherine:	So how many ways have we got? One, two, three, four ... one of these, four, five – right?
David:	Right.
Katherine:	Are there any other ways?
Colin:	One, two, three, four, five.
Katherine:	Hang on, can I use that ruler, David? Eh ... there's another one.
Colin:	We've got five ways ... can do it ...
Katherine:	Yeah ... but you can use loads of shapes and it's still be in half. Yeah ... yeah ... because loads of shapes you can do, loads of shapes can be done ... no, in fact, we've got six ... one, two, three, four, five, six.

Apart from the word 'accurate' introduced into the conversation by the teacher, this example shows little of the three children's mathematical vocabulary or of the actual sharing of ideas. We assume they were showing each other the shapes that they cut and measured, but most of the talk tells a listener very little about what is going on. The children are putting all their efforts into the thinking that will solve the problem. Their discussion supports that thinking. This would certainly not be an occasion to point out the lack of social skills. In fact, if learning is the purpose of the discussion, it is vitally important that children talk in the language or dialect with which they think and feel most comfortable.

It is not always possible when involved with cognitive tasks to talk with others. When writing, for example, a youngster may be completely absorbed in his developing ideas – lost in a world of his own – but still needing to make comments aloud. Teachers must be aware of the needs of some learners to talk to themselves while working – that they may mutter, comment and exclaim to themselves, particularly as they engage in tasks that demand concentrated thinking. There are many reasons why having individual children talking aloud to themselves in busy primary classrooms is impractical – not least because it disturbs other, possibly quieter, learners. However, we must try to find ways of balancing the needs of *all* learners and the 'chunterers' deserve consideration along with the rest.

Final soliloquy

As I write this chapter – on my own, with no noise apart from the buzz of the computer – I am constantly interrupting the silence by reading aloud to myself, making comments about the writing, making remarks that show how I feel, telling myself when I may stop and have a coffee, etc. First sign of madness? In my case, perhaps more likely now than it was fifty years ago, but I suspect I am not alone in indulging in these monologues. There are many other adults and children out there chatting away to the empty air as they work. Children lost in their thoughts, who need to articulate their learning outside organised discussion, will always be part of our classrooms. All the requirements of the National Curriculum for the social aspects of speaking and listening deserve careful planning and teaching, but it is vital that teachers also plan for occasions when children can talk about what they are learning. On these occasions, whether they are social interactions or monologues, youngsters should feel confident to take part, knowing that what matters about talking is not how they sound but what they think.

References

Barnes, D. (1992) 'The role of talk in learning', in Norman, K. (ed.) *Thinking Voices: the work of the National Oracy Project*, 123–8. Sevenoaks: Hodder & Stoughton.

Barnes, D., Britton, J. and Rosen, H. (1971) *Language, the Learner and the School.* Harmondsworth: Penguin.

Britton, J. (1970) *Language and Learning.* London: Penguin.

Bruner, J. (1988) 'Vygotsky: a historical and conceptual perspective', in Mercer, N. (ed.) *Language and Literacy from an Educational Perspective. Volume 1: Language studies,* 86–98. Milton Keynes: Open University Press.

Cazden, C. (1988) 'Social interaction as scaffold: the power and limits of a metaphor' in Lightfoot, M. and Martin, N. (eds) *The Word for Teaching is Learning,* 3–13. Oxford: Heinemann Educational.

DES (1975) *A Language for Life* (The Bullock Report). London: HMSO.

DES and QCA (1999) *The National Curriculum: Handbook for Primary Teachers in England: Key Stages 1 and 2.* London: DfEE and QCA.

Nelson, K. (1996) *Language in Cognitive Development.* Cambridge: Cambridge University Press.

Piaget, J. (1959) *The Language and Thought of the Child,* 3rd edn. London: Routledge and Keegan Paul.

Vygotsky, L. (1988) (translation newly revised and edited by Alex Kozulin) *Thought and Language*. Cambridge, Mass.: The Massachusetts Institute of Technology.

Weir, R. H. (1962) *Language of the Crib*. The Hague: Mouton.

Wells, G. (1987) *The Meaning Makers*. London: Hodder & Stoughton.

Video

Bale, P. and Acland, R. (compilers) (1988) *Talking sense: oracy group work in the primary classroom*. Cumbria County Council.

Part 2

Across the whole curriculum

Chapter 5

Small children talking their way into being readers
Judith Graham

Those of you reading this book will probably be sitting at a desk, in a seat on a vehicle of some sort, in an armchair or possibly lying in bed. You will also probably be alone or if not alone you will not be expecting or even wanting to talk to the persons around you about what you are reading, or at least not immediately. For most of us, reading is largely, unless we particularly choose it not to be so, an activity conducted in silence and alone physically though we may of course not feel lonely as we engage in an interior discourse with another person's written words.

It is not quite like this for young children. Readings are shared between several participants; usually an adult who performs the voice on the page and a child or children who comment, ask and answer questions and perhaps take over the reading. Talk precedes, accompanies and follows the reading and indeed, the reading and the talk surrounding it can sometimes be impossible to disentangle, as children spill forth their responses, predictions and reflections. This is as it should be – a social situation in which contributions mix and mingle to create an enriching experience that lays the foundation for and confirms children's inner voices, convinces them of the power of reading and develops in them, we hope, the wish to possess this power for themselves.

I have been visiting a reception classroom to listen to how children and their teacher read together and talk about literature when the children are new to school and often new to the idea of sitting together to listen to and talk about books. The class I visited was in a school in a rather bleak area of south-east London. Different moments in the classroom are described: the first four are with the whole class; the fifth is with a group and the sixth is with an individual child. The teacher is Rachel Smith. She is an experienced teacher. In the commentary I provide after the episodes, some of the principles on which she bases her literature teaching and some of the practices that she employs are discussed.

Reception

Episode One – whole class

A reception class has been sharing books and other reading matter, including a news-paper, for some 20 minutes after a wet lunchtime. Their teacher calls them together onto the carpet.

'Now,' she says, holding up *A Dark, Dark Tale* by Ruth Brown.

'I know that book,' calls out Daniel. The teacher looks at him and puts her finger on her lips.

'I'm going to read this book to you. It's very similar to this book which we know well don't we?' She holds up *In a Dark, Dark Wood* (Story Chest). 'But there are some differ-ences. See if you can spot them.'

The teacher starts to read. Children start to comment immediately.

'Keep the things in your head and tell us at the end,' she says.

One child excitedly points out the 'things the spider goes on'. Daniel identifies them as spiders' webs.

'Or cobwebs,' adds another child.

The teacher senses the string of comments building up so drops her voice to a whis-per, building up the tension. Ben calls out 'mouse' as the climax is reached. The teacher looks at him and puts her finger on her lips.

'What did you all think would be at the end?' Most of the children expected a ghost as in the earlier book.

'Do you remember how you felt before as you were reading the little book?'

'It gave us a fright.'

'Scared.'

'We got a shock,' adds Ben.

'Yes, we did, didn't we? Now what about your feelings at the end of this book? You've been waiting patiently Dale. What did you feel?'

'Well not scared really. Rather nice.'

'And Tara?'

'I wasn't scared either.'

'I agree with you both. I felt it was a surprise but I wasn't scared, perhaps because I knew the other book. Now I'm going to put these two books in the group reading basket and you can come at any time to see how many things are the same and how many are different in the two books.'

Episode Two – whole class

The class reads *Titch* by Pat Hutchins. 'It's one of our favourites isn't it?' They remem-ber the story well.

'His seed grew massive,' says one child.

'What a good word to describe the plant,' commends the teacher.

'Titch was sad,' says another.

'Why was Titch sad?'

'He wanted to be bigger.'

The teacher shows the illustration of the family on their bikes.

'I've got a massive bike,' says one child. A chorus of claims and counter claims is unleashed.

'I holded nails once,' says a child, changing the subject. 'I didn't like it.'
'There's the fat flower pot.'
'Is it fatter than me?' wonders (plump) Ben.
'Them two are laughing at Titch. They're snooty.'

The teacher questions them further on the feelings of the various characters, edging them towards considering the older two as perhaps thoughtless rather than deliberately mean. At the last page, Daniel is reminded of *Jasper's Beanstalk* (Nick Butterworth and Mick Inkpen) and that book is brought and compared. Memories of a Jack and the Beanstalk panto are shared and then the class is dismissed to work on their separate life-size portraits of the characters and the beanstalk.

Episode Three – whole class

There are 33 children in a very small room on a very hot day.

'Now I know it's a very hot day but when I read the story, I don't want any yawning and sighing. And no fiddling with shoes. Shoes are not important in story time.'
She commends various children who are 'ready to be good listeners' and the rest come into line. She reminds an enthusiastic class of Mary Hoffman and Caroline Binch's *Amazing Grace* and holds up the sequel *Grace & Family*. Several children are flabbergasted that another story with the same character exists. She starts reading and after the first two pages stops to summarise the story so far.
'Grace is really missing her father, isn't she? And in stories, it's always the youngest who is the favourite. Now that Grace's Dad is married again, she won't be the youngest any more.'
She continues the reading. When *Snow White* is mentioned, several children say, 'I've got that!'
The teacher makes links with *Amazing Grace* where Grace's love of traditional stories is well established. As the pages are turned, various children are nominated to voice their responses.
'She's crying there.'
'No, she's playing.'
The teacher stops to dwell on the picture of the market.
'If you've been to Woolwich market, you'll see some things the same but many things different.' Lots of children comment. Later, when Grace has to choose some material, the children are asked to think about which they would choose. Towards the end of the book, when Grace is close to the end of her time with her father in Africa, she is taken to see crocodiles and to make a wish. The illustration is of rather inert and colourless crocodiles. One child puts up her hand to ask if they are dead.
'No. They're not dead,' the teacher says. 'What do you think her wish will be?'
'That the crocodiles will change into a bright colour!' is the child's reply. Other children say that she'll wish to stay in Africa.
'Well, let's see,' says the teacher and the book is finished. Some of the newest reception children are very drowsy and one child is fast asleep. The parents are waiting outside for them. Two black children ask to look at the book again.

Episode Four – whole class

The teacher introduces a new book to the whole class by 'one of my favourite authors, Mike Inkpen'. The book, *If I Had a Pig*, is an accumulative text of the various activities that the small narrator would enjoy with a pet pig, if only he had one. The illustrations give emotional depth and extra detail to a simple text. The class gives the book undivided attention and many children comment. Their comments are acknowledged if the children have raised their hands.

'I've got a pig – a chocolate pig.'
'The pig is standing up.'
'That piggy's getting all messed up.'
'The water's overflowed.'
'That's a cheeky grin on the pig's face.'
'He's hanging the flannel on his nose.'

Samantha sees that the pig plays the role of a teddy bear to the child in the final illustration. The teacher encourages them to count the cake candles to work out the age of the birthday pig and she makes links with the 'house' some children have made under a table and the playhouse in the playground.

The teacher then asks the children to enter 'thinking time'. She writes on the flip chart, 'If you had an animal, what would it be?' Ben and Dale offer answers to the question, choosing a bull and a giraffe respectively. Both boys focus on the games they'd play with their animals and on how they would dress up as these animals. Ben says his bull would 'paw the ground and have a ring in his nose.' The class is asked to go on using their thinking time to imagine their animal.

Episode Five – group

A group is with the teacher on the carpet for group reading. She has ready five copies of *Our Cat Flossie* by Ruth Brown. She appoints Dale to distribute them, one to each child.

'Move back all of you so that you are in a circle round me and so that the book lies flat on the floor. Keep the book closed and look carefully at the cover. Point at the first word of the title, all of you. And now at the name of the author.'

A non-group child interrupts and is reminded not to disturb the teacher when she's working with a group.

'Now turn over. Look at the illustration and then put your finger on the first word.'

The teacher begins reading, her finger under each word. Discussion centres on unfriendly neighbours and of how hackles on a dog's back indicate unfriendliness.

'Shall we turn over and find out more about our cat Flossie?' Four children try to interrupt. They are ignored and go away.

'Well done, Heather,' says the teacher. 'You've got your finger on the right place to start reading.'

The teacher reads and the children offer comments on the illustrations.

'Flossie wants to catch the bird and the fish.'
'She's laughing – not helping at all.'
'She ain't helping with the knitting at all.'

The teacher comments, 'It's a trick in the writing for us to enjoy.' There is a long pause.

'She's polishing the shoe with her tail and neck and chin,' murmurs one child.
'I wonder why Flossie hates going to the vet?' asks the teacher.
''Cos she gets squashed in the basket,' replies Heather.
''Cos she hates operations,' says another.

They all look at the picture of Flossie and the Christmas tree.

'She's bashing the decorations and they'll all crack.'

'She likes things that move,' Kara says.

'My cat likes eating grass.'

The teacher dwells on the last picture.

'She looks as if she's very tired, she's had a long day and she's dreaming of all those mischievous things she's done in the day.'

Episode Six – reading with an individual child

The children have a time for free-choice activities, so the teacher has time to read one-to-one with Ben. He chooses *Rosie's Walk* and is reading the written text which the teacher underlines with her finger. He can identify 'haycock' and other isolated words on request; he comments liberally on the illustrations and ensures that his teacher sees such details as the rope around Rosie's leg. At the end of the book and at his teacher's request, Ben identifies letters in his name from a line of the text. All Ben's achievements in this reading conference (noticing and enjoying detail in the pictures, remembering the story line, predicting what is going to happen, identifying words and letters) are enumerated by his teacher and she congratulates him on being a good reader. Ben is keen to read the book again and does so to me (J.G.). He makes sure that I miss nothing in the pictures.

Commentary

Bringing personal experience to bear

If children do not make connections between the lives they live, both physically and emotionally, and the lives portrayed in books, the chances are that books will remain peripheral to their lives. Rachel knows this and it is a part of her philosophy of literature teaching to encourage and accept personal links made by her class. (The practical management of these personal comments is discussed below.) The child who muses: 'I holded nails once – I didn't like it' makes *Titch* a more significant text for himself and the child who gives us her cat's habits, 'My cat likes eating grass', comes to know that it is of such detail that Ruth Brown can make a story. Rachel will invite children to remember, for instance, their trips to Woolwich market, so that Grace's African outing can be seen as both familiar and strange. During the various book-related activities that the children engage in after reading, they make frequent 'life to literature and literature to life' references.

Making connections with other books

This is the second plank of Rachel's literature teaching strategies. The common, class-shared, social experience of books read gives everybody a chance to make connections. Rachel often chooses books (as in the two 'jump' stories in Episode One) because they are connected in some way. They either share a theme, authorship, illustrator or some aspect of plot or characterisation. There is clear evidence that children's enjoyment and interest is ensured if they sense and can identify these connections. This was most dramatic when they exclaimed at the concept of Grace (from *Amazing Grace*) appearing in another title, *Grace & Family*, and although the sequel is a more complex book for children of this age, they followed the reading with intense interest. (Here, perhaps, is some early indication of the pull of the series.) It is not only Rachel who chooses books because they can be linked; children are starting to volunteer cross-references as when *Jasper's Beanstalk* is remembered during a reading of *Titch*. Children also make connections to books they have at home and to shows they have seen.

A community of readers

Another strategy that Rachel uses, deliberately and methodically, is to help each member of the class feel that they belong to a class which reads books. Into the class' repertoire and memory go certain books; the children have mental ownership of these books and Rachel reminds them of that. 'This is a book we know well', 'It's one of our favourites isn't it?', 'I felt like you did'. She also teaches them to name and value story time – it is a time for listening and responding and nothing is allowed to rob the children of these slots. 'Thinking time' is also a joint ritual that the children understand and use for extending ideas and thoughts about books.

Time for the illustrations

Most reception and infant teachers are wildly enthusiastic about picture books but nevertheless, children look more closely than we do and want to say what they see in the illustrations. Rachel remembers to give time for children to look and comment. It may be that children name the items in the picture: 'those are spiders' webs'; 'she's crying there'; 'the water's overflowed'; 'he's hanging a flannel on his nose'. It may be that they start to interpret illustrations. Samantha comments that the pig is a substitute teddy bear for the child and Dale reflects that Flossie 'ain't helping with the knitting at all' and several children discuss what the raised hairs on the back of the unfriendly neighbouring dog might mean. Rachel may aid their deductions as when she invites them to count the birthday candles to work out the age of the pig. Even when the focus is on the written text (as in the group reading session described above), there is no rush to turn over the page before the illustrations have been read, details selected and their contribution absorbed.

Reading aloud

Rachel recognises that she will need to read and re-read several times a day if she is to build up her children's stock of stories, so that their minds grow full of dramas and images. Only when they know stories really well will they seek them out and give themselves the private lessons that turn them into readers. Her voice carries the written content while the class fixes on the pictures. She is skilled at dropping her voice to create tension, at 'doing the voices' of the different characters and of reading rhythmically those texts which have in-built repetition and pattern which is so helpful to early readers. After only one or two readings, her class can echo the heavy beats that are repeated in *A Dark, Dark Tale* or imitate the rising intonation of 'and Titch's seed grew and grew and grew' in *Titch*. Rachel reminds her children that the books are kept in a certain place for later perusal thus increasing the chances of children 'reciting' (often using her intonation) well-known stories until they are reading for themselves.

As part of her reading aloud strategy, Rachel will offer summaries and explanations at those points where the text is perhaps a bit difficult (as in *Grace & Family*) or at the end of a story where she wants to encapsulate both the book's message and the children's memories. 'Flossie looks as if she's very tired, she's had a long day and she's dreaming of all those mischievous things she's done in the day.' At other times, the reading will be given without interruptions so that the children make a total entry into the secondary world of story.

The affective side of reading

There are two aspects of this important component of Rachel's literature teaching. There is the invitation to recall their own feelings on hearing a story and there is the encouragement to identify the emotions experienced by the protagonists in the stories. The instinctive sympathy that children show towards characters ('Titch is sad') is something to value and encourage.

'Them two are laughing at Titch. They're snooty.' On this occasion, the teacher takes the opportunity to extend their understanding of the range and complexity of feelings and suggests that insensitivity rather than malice is the problem. Frequently, the exploration of characters' feelings draws on the life experiences the children may have had ('I wonder why Flossie hates going to the vet?') or she names emotions that the children may well know about ('Grace is really missing her father').

Explicit teaching

A major part of Rachel's explicit teaching about decoding written language is done in whole-class sessions on writing. When, for instance, she wrote on the flip chart, 'If you had an animal, what would it be?' the children gave undivided attention to the words arriving in front of them and then read and re-read the sentence with Rachel. In group sessions, there are also opportunities to talk about such basic things as books being for finding out about the lives of characters, the pages of a book being turned at the right point, and the place you must look at when you start reading a page. Teaching the terms is explicitly done in the group time: 'author', 'title' and 'illustration' are used frequently. 'Distinctive' words like 'haycock' can be savoured and individual letters identified and discussed. All of this teaching is interwoven with praise – 'what a good word to describe the plant' and 'well done – you've got your finger under the word where I need to start reading'.

Choice of texts

Rachel is an experienced teacher. She knows which books are sure-fire hits with this age group. But because she is a reader herself, she wants to share her favourites with the class, thereby demonstrating that part of being a reader is developing favourite books. She shares new books with her class and she is guided here by knowing the author or illustrator and liking their work, by her own delight in the book and by her appreciation that the book has a depth or multi-layered richness to it. Look at the talk that is engendered by *Our Cat Flossie*. The children appreciate the joke being worked out in this book and the text itself gives the teacher a chance to develop both a taste for such wit and an understanding about how it is achieved. 'A trick for us to enjoy' – the children don't comment further on Rachel's explanation but there is space for reflection. Teachers cannot always predict what children are going to find intriguing or special in a book – who could have thought that the children would have worried about the crocodiles being dead in *Grace & Family?* – but the book's very complexity makes it one that children want to talk about. Rachel is aware also of the importance of providing books that reflect a multicultural society. The fascination that *Grace & Family* exerted over two children in her class suggests that they were enjoying a book where they saw images of black children like themselves.

Children into pupils

In order to teach anything, a teacher has to induct children into the ground rules of the classroom. Conveying expectations, insisting on adherence and remaining consistent make the business of teaching a great deal more manageable than it would otherwise be.

In the case of literature, the teacher has to induct her class into the ways of listening to and talking about books. One of the questions she asks to which children unfailingly respond is, 'Are you ready to be good listeners?' But children new to school are forever calling out their thoughts during the reading (not a problem in one-to-one reading) and although reminders about putting up one's hand have been made since day one, many find this a hard rule to learn. To those who forget, a telling look, a finger on the lips and a reminder seem to do the trick. Rachel uses eye contact and gesture effectively so that the general flow is not interrupted by reprimands. But children want to tell and want to comment and Rachel knows the importance of this so the promise 'we'll hear your thoughts at the end' is made and kept. Another strategy she uses is to give a child, who wants to spill the beans and reveal how the story ends, a conspiratorial look as if to say – 'yes, you and I together know – let's keep our secret'.

As the term progresses, the more overarching message – that books are for us to enjoy and to talk about together – becomes more overt and widely understood and we see the children managing to read together and talk together in groups without the teacher.

Conclusion

The teacher of this reception class saw her role as crucial at the start of these young children's literary lives. All their subsequent expectations of how they will be listened to and encouraged to share their thoughts have their roots in their classroom experience here. Rachel starts from her own strengths: interest in children's thoughts, knowledge of books, delight in language, confidence to let the sessions be truly open-ended and interactive. All of this means that the children grow in curiosity, confidence, literary and critical ability. Her approach is based on three essential impulses:

- to find, read aloud and 'give' to the children the wealth of great stories that are created for them;
- to create frequent opportunities for children in which she can guide and the children can offer responses (of how stories make them feel, of how they remind them of other books and events and people, of how stories are constructed, of how illustrations play a part);
- to help children value being part of a literate community within which it is only a matter of time before they are reading for themselves.

You will notice that there is no mention of *The National Curriculum* nor of *The National Literacy Strategy* here. This is not to denounce those two documents but they are essentially programmes of instruction. It is time to consider approaching the teaching of literature (and thus of literacy) in ways which are more philosophical and principled but also more directly derived from enabling classroom practice.

References

Brown, R. (1981) *A Dark, Dark Tale*. London: Andersen Press.
Brown, R. (1986) *Our Cat Flossie*. London: Andersen Press.
Butterworth, N. and Inkpen, M. (1991) *Jasper's Beanstalk*. London: Hodder & Stoughton.
Hoffman, M. and Binch, C. (1991) *Amazing Grace*. London: Frances Lincoln.
Hoffman, M. and Binch, C. (1995) *Grace & Family*. London: Frances Lincoln.
Hutchins, P. (1970) *Rosie's Walk*. London: The Bodley Head.
Hutchins, P. (1971) *Titch*. London: The Bodley Head.
Inkpen, M. (1988) *If I Had A Pig*. London: Hodder & Stoughton.
Story Chest (1981) *In a Dark, Dark Wood*. London: Kingscourt.

Chapter 6

Talking about reading
George Hunt

Background

The potential benefits of the talk that occurs when children converse with adults or with other children about their reading have been indicated in a number of studies. Snow (1983) shows that parent–child reading interactions enhance understanding of differences between interpersonal speech and decontextualised book language. Wells (1995), in her study of 'grand conversations' between pupils in literature discussion groups, indicates how such conversations enable participants to integrate literary and personal experience. Corson (2000) presents an array of conversations demonstrating how knowledge about language and the ability to use such knowledge is developed through literature-based dialogue.

What all of these case studies emphasises is the value of the flexible, non-oppressive routine. Talk unfolds according to predictable procedures which keep the conversation within broad bounds without constraining expression or participation. When adults contribute, they do so in order to guide discussion, or simply share ideas, rather than to dominate or direct. The talk is exploratory rather than aimed at the 'ventriloquisation' of predetermined knowledge.

In recent years, the educational establishment's insistence on prescriptive curricula and measurable outcomes has demonstrated the vulnerability of exploratory talk. The vagaries of such talk, not to mention the time that it takes away from direct teaching, are barely tolerated under a regime which values a 'sense of urgency' in classrooms (DfEE 1998, p. 8) and the necessity of having everybody 'working to the same blueprint' (DfEE 1997, p. 20). The National Literacy Strategy, which has transformed the teaching of literacy in England, although advocating that literacy teaching should involve lively discussion of texts, emphasises in all of its documentation that the teacher should carefully police such discussion to ensure that it does not stray from the prescribed objectives (see for example 'Directing Discussion' DfEE 1999). Most of the teacher–pupil interactions featured in its training videos conform to the Initiation–Response–Evaluation (IRE) pattern long recognised as a typical, and intrinsically limiting, form of classroom interaction (Stubbs 1975). This pattern, illustrated in the transcript below, sets up a pseudo-dialogue in which the teacher's role is to elicit prior knowledge and to reward its regurgitation, while limiting the child's language to brief responses to convergent questions.

A group of children in a guided reading session are looking at a book under the direction of a teacher who is conducting a demonstration lesson for a colleague.

Teacher: Now on that page there's a word that's got two words in it. Can you find
           it for me? We call it a compound word. Two words together. Have you
           found it Adam?
Child: Moonlight.
Teacher: Is he right? Are there two words in that word? Let's see everybody's finger
           underneath it. Right. What's the first word?
Group: Moon.
Teacher: And what's the last word?
Group: Light.
Teacher: Good.

(Literacy Training Pack, Video 1, DfEE 1998)

The teacher clearly directs and dominates here. Her turns are more frequent, lengthy
and complex than those of the children, and her implicit objective is to closely restrict
what the children actually say in response to the text. Although such exchanges can
contribute to assessment and perhaps, if made more expansive, provide insight into children's thinking, they are unlikely to produce the richer benefits of talk outlined above.

In seeking alternatives to the IRE pattern, educational researchers and practitioners have
often emphasised the differences and discontinuities between conversations at home and
at school. Investigations of adult–child interactions at home which seem to facilitate
language development have indicated the following features as being potentially beneficial:

- Joint focus of attention: adult and child converse about a stimulus which is mutually
  interesting (Snow and Goldfield 1983).
- Symmetrical conversational rights: the adult does not dominate the conversation, but
  instead supports the child's participation (Wells 1981).
- Responsiveness of adult speech to that of the child: the adult's contributions may be
  'finely tuned' to the linguistic capacity of the child, or they may be pitched somewhat
  beyond the child's current ability, persuading the child to adapt to more rigorous
  communicative demands (Richards and Gallaway 1999).

Underlying these features is the simple but powerful concept of *contingency*: children's
talk is responded to in ways that show the child that the adult is interested in what he or
she has said. The adult may recast the child's utterance in a different grammatical form, or
expand the utterance, or extend the topic initiated by the child. Richards (1990), while
taking a cautious view of applications of child language research to pedagogy, suggests
that the evidence that such contingent responses contribute to language development is a
finding which is important for teachers. 'In effective and mutually rewarding conversations,
adult interlocutors work at interpreting meaning, sustaining the topic and passing the
conversational turn without forcing the child into a passively responsive mode' (p. 19).

Such conversations are rare at school. Wells (1981, 1986), using data from the Bristol
Study of Language Development, has shown that, in comparison with the opportunities
that they have at home, children in school take fewer conversational turns, express a
narrower range of meanings, ask fewer questions, and are far less likely to initiate
conversations with adults. Similar findings are reported by Tizard and Hughes (1984).
The restrictions on some classroom conversations, and the pressures which give rise to
these restrictions, are illustrated in the following extract:

Teacher: Darren's gone to his new class in school.
Child: My sister …
Teacher: Your sister – has she gone into a new class or into a new school?
Child: New school.

Teacher: She's gone into the junior school? Well isn't that lovely? She's got a new uniform ... she's got a new jumper? Or has she got a cardigan?

Child: Cardie.

Teacher: Lovely. Lovely! Nigel, would you like an apple? Anybody like more milk? Anybody want a piece of apple? No? All right. Wouldn't you like to drink yours up like Jason? Would you like to drink your milk all up like Jason's doing? Any more? Good girl. You've got new shoes, have you? What colour are they, Chatinder? What colour are Chatinder's shoes? Can you remember? Can you say that? Say it then.

Child: Black.

Teacher: Black. Good girl.

(Willes 1978)

As Willes points out, we never learn what the child, bravely making an initiation, wanted to say about her sister. Instead, the teacher, in the course of dealing with a flurry of chores, unwittingly forces the child into the response slot in a ritualistic IRE sequence, her contribution reduced to a single word answer to a trivial question.

It is clear that such exchanges are inevitable in situations where a teacher is dealing single-handedly with a wide range of demands from a large number of children. The management of behaviour and the detailed pedagogic agenda exclude many opportunities for contingent responses to child initiations. A teacher attempting to provide individualised topic-extending responses to such initiations would have to abandon a mandated timetable and an orderly classroom. The challenge for teachers is to find ways of integrating opportunities for contingency rich talk into a brief and increasingly prescribed school day. In the remainder of this chapter, I will outline two simple, flexible routines, centred on literacy, which might help teachers to do this.

The anti-pedagogical reading conference

In spite of the marginalisation of the practice of hearing individual children read brought about by the National Literacy Strategy, many schools still devote time to this task, often delegating it to trained or untrained assistants and volunteers. At first sight, the individual reading conference would appear to be a promising context for rich conversation. Ideally, the child and adult share a stimulating focus of attention; the child takes the initiative by reading from and commenting evaluatively or appreciatively on the text; the adult responds contingently by expanding, recasting or extending both the words the child reads and the observations that he or she makes in creating links between the text and his or her own experiences. Unfortunately, these opportunities for open-ended conversation about child-initiated topics are often overshadowed by a concern with teaching word level skills and assessing the reader's competence. Hunt and Richards (in press) for example, in analysing ten Key Stage 1 reading conversations, found that both teachers and parent volunteers assumed almost complete control over reading conversations, and were preoccupied with directing the child's thought and language towards accurate reproduction of the text. Children made very few life-to-text links or evaluative comments, and when they did so, adults tended to hasten the child's attention back to word level decoding. The following exchange demonstrates this:

The child has been looking at an illustration in a book about birds showing an X-ray photo of a chick embryo in the egg, and the teacher has compared it to a human embryo.

Child:	Does it start off with just the head?
Adult:	A human baby?
Child:	Yes.
Adult:	It starts off as a tiny ... cell, and then it gets bigger. I'm not sure whether the head comes first or all the parts gradually develop. [refocusing on text] All ...
Child:	All birds have babies.
Adult:	No, look, it doesn't start with buh does it?
Child:	ffff ...

Here we have a very promising opportunity for a more open conversation. The adult has initiated a life-to-text link by comparing chick and human embryos, and the child takes over the topic by making her own initiation in the form of a 'real' question; that is, one to which the answer is genuinely not known. Such questions are comparatively rare in educational discourse, but they are clearly very effective in sustaining and elaborating conversation. The teacher's response is informative, and, by acknowledging her own uncertainty, she provides a stimulus for further joint speculation or discussion about where to seek further information. However, the opportunity for elaborating the conversation is sacrificed to the demands of teaching and assessing word level skills. The child's miscue when her attention is redirected to the page might be read as evidence that her imagination is still preoccupied with the preceding topic.

It is important to acknowledge that both the teaching and the assessment of word level skills are essential, but the National Literacy Strategy already provides daily, intensive word level teaching within the literacy hour, and a perhaps superfluous wealth of opportunities for assessment. What is missing is the space for loosely structured talk around a focus of attention selected by the child. I would suggest therefore, that alongside the experiences offered by the literacy hour, children be allowed, on a regular basis, conversational time with an adult which has *no immediate pedagogical objectives at all*. Assistants and volunteers, who are not as constrained as teachers by a narrow instructional agenda, and who are likely to be less formal in their relationships with children, might well be in a better position than teachers to offer contingency rich conversation focused on a book or other literacy stimulus. There would be no compulsion for the child to read aloud or answer adult initiated questions. The purpose would be merely to chat about the stimulus in the predictable but highly flexible routines that have been shown to characterise language-enhancing book conversations between parents and preschool children (Snow and Goldfield 1983).

The difficulties of establishing such simple routines should not be underestimated. One of the objectives of the National Literacy Strategy is to train classroom assistants to adopt modes of interaction with children which are focused on precise programme objectives. This homogenisation of classroom talk threatens the potential benefits to children of experiencing a range of conversational styles. More fundamentally, perhaps, conversations within literacy events are also shaped by the *child's* beliefs about what kind of talk is expected of him or her. In analysing such conversations, I have found exchanges of the following type to be quite common.

Adult:	What's that word say?
Child:	... the
Adult:	Good girl.
Child:	... the party balloons.
Adult:	No, it's just the balloons. Do you like balloons?

Child:	(nods)
Adult:	Well I'm afraid I don't. I don't like balloons at all in fact.
	(pause)
Child:	(reads) ... the balloons.

Here the adult makes a life-to-text link by volunteering some personal information related to the theme of the book. It is obvious from the context that she has a piece of autobiography to share, and she pauses in order to allow the child to probe her remark. The child, however, ignores this prompt and returns to the customary business of reproducing the text. It is clear that persuading children to converse about books is not the straightforward job it might seem (Greenhough and Hughes 1999). What is needed is early, frequent and consistent engagement in such conversation, so that children come to see talking informally about their reading as an integral part of school experience (Chambers 1977).

Guided issues-based discussion

One-to-one conversations between adults and children in educational settings are rare. More frequently, the teacher engages with whole classes, or organises activities for smaller groups with varying degrees of adult intervention. As mentioned above, the potential of group discussion for developing both literacy and oral language is well documented; but so too, are the anxieties felt by teachers in allowing children the latitude for self-directed discussion. The independent or guided group work segment of the literacy hour provides a daily opportunity for children to engage in discussion, but in a recent informal survey of attitudes towards the literacy hour amongst over 100 students at my own institution, the most common concern was the need to 'keep children on task' during this period, whilst avoiding vapid 'pin-down' activities whose main purpose is to keep children quietly occupied while the teacher gets on with teaching another group.

What is needed, again, are routines which are predictable enough to structure group activity, while remaining flexible enough to allow for reflection and interaction. Tasks in which children compare viewpoints on ethical issues embedded in texts can provide such flexible routines. Contingency rich conversation is promoted by the teacher assigning a problem for which there is no preordained correct solution, but which is focused and engaging enough to frame the discussion within manageable bounds. Opportunities for contingency emerge from the need for participants to listen to other contributions, then to question, clarify or contradict what has been said, revisiting and reinterpreting the text in the process. To illustrate this, a brief excerpt from a discussion based on a narrative text called 'Anna's Story' (Hunt 1999) is presented below. This is an adapted folk-tale in which a woman living a solitary life in a forest obtains a husband after stealing the feathers of a bird-man, thus trapping him in human form. After the couple have started a family, the bird-man discovers his stolen feathers and deserts his wife and young children forever. The group have been asked to discuss whether or not Anna should have stolen the feathers. (Later, they were asked to discuss the morality of the bird-man's departure, and to consider whether their judgements would have been different if the genders of the protagonists were reversed, as they are in the 'selkie' story on which the narrative is based.)

Child 1:	Well, she wasn't lonely any more, not even when he flew away.
Child 2:	How do you know she wasn't? It says she was upset.

Child 3:   No it doesn't. It says the children were crying. She wasn't.
Child 1:   But she wasn't lonely anymore because she had some children to help her
           now.
Teacher: So does that mean that she was right to steal the feathers, because it meant
           she wasn't lonely?
Child 2 and Child 3: No.
Child 1:   Well I bet you'd do it if you were that lonely.

Here, Child 1 asserts a pragmatic judgement that Anna has solved her main problem in spite of the story's sad ending. Child 2 does not challenge such pragmatism, but disputes 1's interpretation of the text. Child 2 in turn is challenged by 3 who offers a reminder of what the text actually said, rather than implied. Child 1 now picks up 3's reference to the children to support the claim in her first utterance. The teacher attempts to reinstate the ethical dimension of the discussion, prompting 1's invitation for the teacher to feel empathy with Anna. Each turn builds on meanings expressed in previous turns, and the text is subjected to re-scrutiny. The teacher acts as a participant rather than a director, and his contributions are shorter and less frequent than those of the children. Throughout this discussion, the children were going beyond the words on the page, making inferences about the feelings and motivations of the characters and projecting themselves into alternative interpretations (nowhere in the text, for example, does it state *explicitly* that Anna felt lonely in the forest, or that she stole the feathers in order to obtain a husband).

In analysing a conversation based on a story called 'Blue Riding Hood' (Hunt 1995), a version of the familiar folk-tale rewritten to undermine the reader's expectations of the characters' personalities, Skidmore (2000) points out similar outcomes. The children have been asked to put the characters in the story in order of blame, a task again without a predetermined correct outcome. The task channels the discussion, which consists largely of child–child contingent exchanges, the order of participation determined by the participants themselves. Skidmore claims that by pooling their interpretations and hypotheses about the story, the group are enabled to engage in more speculative thinking than would have been afforded by the kind of individual and convergent responses demanded by traditional comprehension activities.

It is useful for such discussions to be 'chaired' by the teacher, or by another adult, when they are first introduced, but an appropriate goal would be the gradual withdrawal of teacher intervention. This type of discussion need not, of course, be confined to discussion of folk-tales or even to fiction. History and contemporary life abound in examples of issues, plights and predicaments which lend themselves to this approach, which might constitute a useful bridge between literacy education and education for citizenship.

Conclusion

Talk which evolves under low constraints towards indeterminate outcomes might appear to be a liberal luxury in a world of termly objectives and numerical targets for test results. However, it seems clear that such talk does have a large and neglected potential for enhancing learning. The problem is finding the time, and the confidence, to allow learners to ask their own questions and seek their own answers.

References

Chambers, A. (1977) *Booktalk*. London: The Bodley Head.

Corson, R. (2000) *Literacy and learning through talk*. Buckingham: Open University Press.

DfEE (1997) *The Implementation of the National Literacy Strategy*. London: DfEE.

DfEE (1998) *The National Literacy Strategy: Framework for Teaching*. London: DfEE.

DfEE (1999) *The National Literacy Strategy: Training Module 1: Teaching and Learning Strategies*. London: DfEE.

Greenhough, P. and Hughes, M. (1999) 'Encouraging conversing: trying to change what parents do when their children read with them', *Reading* **33**(3), 98–105.

Hunt, G. (1995) *Curriculum Bank: Reading*. Leamington Spa: Scholastic.

Hunt, G. (1999) *Further Curriculum Bank: Reading*. Leamington Spa: Scholastic.

Hunt, G. and Richards, B. (in press) 'Beyond the words on the page: the reading conference as a forum for language development', in Smith, P. (ed.) *Talking Classrooms: Shaping children's learning through oral language instruction*. Newark, Del: International Reading Association.

Richards, B. (1990) 'Access to the agenda: some observations on language development research and its relevance for the practitioner', *Australian Journal of Remedial Education* **22**, 16–20.

Richards, B. and Gallaway, C. (1999) 'Language acquisition in children: input and interaction', in Spolsky, B. (ed.) *Concise encyclopaedia of educational linguistics*. Oxford: Pergamon.

Skidmore, D. (2000) 'From pedagogical dialogue to dialogic pedagogy', *Language in Education* **14**(4).

Snow, C. (1983) 'Literacy and language: Relationships during the pre-school years', *Harvard Educational Review* **53**, 165–9.

Snow, C. and Goldfield, B. (1983) 'Turn the page please: situation-specific language acquisition', *Journal of Child Language* **10**, 551–69.

Stubbs, M. (1975) 'Teaching and talking: a sociolinguistic approach to classroom interaction', in Chanon, G. and Delamont, S. (eds) *Frontiers of Classroom Research*. Slough: NFER.

Tizard, B. and Hughes, M. (1984) *Young Children Learning*. London: Fontana.

Wells, D. (1995) 'Leading grand conversations', in Roser, N. I. and Martinez, M. G. (eds) *Book Talk and Beyond*. Newark, Del: International Reading Association.

Wells, G. (1981) *Learning through interaction: the study of language development*. Cambridge: Cambridge University Press.

Wells, G. (1986) *The Meaning Makers: children learning language and using language to learn*. Portsmouth, NH: Heinemann.

Willes, M. (1978) 'Early lessons learned too well', in Adelman, C. (ed.) *Uttering, muttering*. Reading: Bulmershe College of Higher Education.

Chapter 7

Talking about writing
Joy McCormick

Starting off a piece of writing is rather like getting on a train. Our invitation to children to undertake such a journey however may be flawed if we do not provide them with tickets to enable them to reach their destination. When we start to explore the needs of the learner in engaging with the writing process we begin to realise there are several stages or 'platforms' to travel through in order to produce a piece of work. Each 'platform' within the writing process demands a triangulation of skills, knowledge and understanding, and it is the use of talk in a variety of ways that can support their acquisition and development. The National Writing Project (1986–88) illustrated the value of children gaining responses from each other. Through peer conferencing, for example, children would be able to develop a greater awareness of what could be included in a checklist for successful writing which, in turn, enables them to formulate and articulate their own perceptions of each other's work. Through talking to each other about the composition and construction of a piece of writing children can share experiences and consider what they know and understand. Bereiter and Scardamalia (1987) suggest that children are able to demonstrate compositional maturity through the way they are able to talk with knowledge about their stories. An example of this is found in six-year-old Sophie's comment as she borrows ideas temporarily and develops her own writing craft, 'Will you write the good ideas on the board 'cos I want to use it in my writing.' We could say that as each bit of the learning journey is undertaken by the writer, in discourse with others, a ticket is stamped to ensure the learning is relevant and valid!

The booklet *Teaching Speaking and Listening Skills in Key Stages 1 and 2* (QCA 1999) was produced by the Qualifications and Curriculum Authority to complement the work of the National Literacy Strategy. It provides a whole-school framework and practical guidance that promotes the importance of speaking and listening, especially in relation to writing. The introduction states:

> The objective which suggests that children 'collaborate with others to write stories in chapters' (Y4 T2) involves children using the oral skills of planning together and negotiating content and what each is to do, in order to succeed in their literacy work. ... The links between oral and written language can be encouraged and built on.

While the QCA documentation has been widely welcomed by teachers, their ability to fully read such documentation and to rethink their teaching strategies in response, can be weakened through pressures of time and ever increasing responsibilities. My supporting role of external consultant often involves enabling schools to focus on ideas and approaches being developed across the whole school, and working alongside individual teachers to make sense of it all in the classroom. This chapter shares a case study of my work in partnership with one school in Sunderland where the staff began to make connections between the importance of speaking and listening and writing development as a result of:

- a need to provide learning opportunities that would raise achievement in writing;
- an interest in using partner and group talk to support the writing process;
- a desire to explore strategies suggested in the QCA framework.

Providing opportunities to achieve

Achieving significant improvement in the achievement of writing, particularly for boys, was a long-standing challenge for Barnwell Primary School. The teachers felt the need to adopt an effective strategy that could be used across the key stages. Such a strategy would also become a component of a teaching and learning policy that became a base to support the pedagogy of their teaching. Writing was being taught largely through the literacy hour and the stimulus for it was being sought, on the whole, from the vicarious rather than first hand experiences. They wanted to enrich the motivation to write by using 'talk partners'. The intention was that, as the children became more experienced, the partnerships would gradually develop into more sophisticated group work and involve extended writing and the development of writing across the curriculum. Plans led to a series of sessions with teachers through which we explored and questioned the planning, the teaching, and the children's responses. In all cases, reference to the QCA documentation was made to consider the speaking and listening skills that were being taught and developed.

Working with Key Stage 1

The focus of work in Years 1 and 2 was on traditional tales. We started by establishing rules for working together, for instance rules about taking turns, participating appropriately and contributing to the creation of stories through responding in role. Each partner was either titled 'A' or 'B' to help them structure their discussion. They would take it in turns to say what they felt, whether they agreed with each other, and to add a further comment or question. Key skills to be taught were:

> Listening and responding to a range of suggestions
> Taking different roles in the story
> Making relevant contributions to discussion

Story structure and language was modelled through shared reading:

> Orientation – Opening to the story, e.g. 'Once there was ...'
> Complication – Something happens/there is a problem to be solved
> Resolution – A satisfactory ending

Discussion was aimed at developing the understanding of story structure as children analysed the characters, became involved in a sequence of actions and then completed the story.

Sequence of activities

1. The children revisited a big storybook of the tale of Red Riding Hood. The opening scene was created with a large poster of a dense wood and a range of objects, i.e. dead leaves, bark, twisted twigs, that the children could explore through touch and smell.

Children worked in pairs to come up with effective words that described the scene. The words were written on 'post-its' and placed on the poster. A story map was introduced and the teacher, as narrator, used the story language from the big book in combination with the children's ideas to start retelling the story.

2. The children were given the dilemma of grandmother, ill in bed, and Red Riding Hood needing to travel into the dark wood to help her (a picture of Red Riding Hood's house was added to the map). The children were asked to re-enact the scene with their partner; 'A' was to be mother asking Red Riding Hood to go and explaining why and 'B', Red Riding Hood responding. The teacher intervened to help construct the dialogue between certain children who needed support. Some children were then encouraged to present their responses in role to the rest of the class.

3. The narrator took the feelings of Red Riding Hood into account as she told how the character set off holding a basket full of things that would help the grandmother (footsteps and basket added to map). In pairs, children took it in turns to write a list of possible things in the basket. Teacher scribed a list that combined all their responses on a flip chart.

4. The children were asked to think of something that Red Riding Hood had hidden at the bottom of her basket in case she met the wolf. What could it be? The teacher explained that she couldn't fit an axe into her basket so it must be something else. Each pair added their thoughts to the bottom of their list. (At this point grandmother's cottage was added to the map with footsteps travelling through some trees – children were reminded of the words used earlier to describe the wood.)

5. The narrator then continued, 'As she draws near the cottage where her grandmother lives how does she begin to feel? What can she hear? What can she see?' Children worked in pairs again in the following way:

6. Child A shut their eyes and thought of the questions that had been asked. When touched by child B, child A had to say what they felt, saw and heard (for example, 'Leaves scrunched like walking on snowflakes' – was one reply.) Partners A and B then exchanged roles.

•7. To end the story, Red Riding Hood opened the door to the cottage. Further questions were asked: Will she meet the wolf or won't she? What will she do if she does? Do you remember what she has hidden in her basket? Children were asked to decide on their own ending to the story – some story language sentence starts were provided from the book to help. They were encouraged to take it in turns to write and consider how they might support and check each other's work.

8. Finally, children had a go at retelling the story with the help of everyone else and the map. When the story came to the end, the different sets of partners surprised everyone with what they had in the basket to use against the wolf and how the tale ended! In one case, the wolf had his tail pinned to the floor with a drawing pin while Red Riding Hood threw a large net over him!

Working with Key Stage 2

The pupils in Year 3 had been looking at non-fiction texts for two weeks. The children had been asked to research a topic on one of the following – deserts, oceans, rivers or volcanoes. The aim was for the children to prepare presentations for a school assembly from what they had learned. Children worked in pairs reflecting on and refining their work as well as extending their ideas. Visual and written frames provided a support for an oral presentation.

Sequence of activities

1. Each child produced a visual representation of what they had learnt in their independent research work. The picture was shared with their partner, and turns were taken to listen to each other and then give a comment.

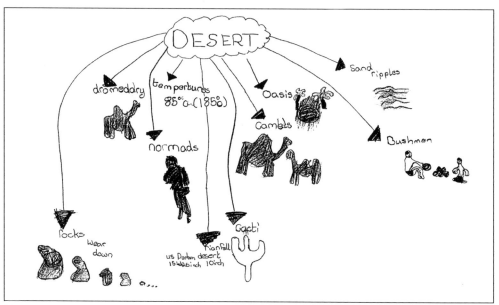

Figure 7.1

2. Pictures were exchanged with another pair. The new pictures were considered and they were encouraged to ask questions about; anything they would like further information about, something they were not sure about, something important they felt should be there but was not or vocabulary they were unsure of.

3. Children moved into groups of four to listen to each other's questions. They were encouraged to ensure that everyone in the group had to answer a question. If someone didn't know the answer, other people in the group could help them.

4. A prompt sheet was produced on a large flip chart with the help of the children. Prompts included:

> Have we included the important points?
> Is our work clear or will it need further explanation?
> Are there some interesting facts?

5. Report/talk frame introduced alongside the above prompts. Children worked on their own frame using 'sentence starts' to guide them.

6. In pairs, children reviewed their work and considered whether extra resources were needed. Children used sections of their pictures alongside the relevant parts of their reports to help them remember.

As result of the work on non-fiction, the children were inspired to write stories based upon the information they had gained during their topic. The following brief extracts are from two of the stories:

Journey to a volcano
All I could see was blue as the boat I was travelling on rocked on the cold water. We were heading for an island famous for its dormant volcano. As we got closer to land I saw a big volcano and I heard a loud bang. I jumped with shock. Smoke began to fill the sky. I saw balls of black ash blast out of the crater, sparks of fire were splurting and the red and yellow lava was running down the sides of the mountain.

A day on the river
'This is a moderate flow river,' informed Mam, just as a kingfisher swooped over our heads.
   'Can we feed the ducks,' pleaded my brother anxiously. There were many plants there. My favourite was the crowfoot.

Providing structures for writing

Classroom experiences described in this chapter provide examples of and extensions to Lilian Katz's reflections on how young children should be learning:

> Interaction that arises in the course of activity provides a context for much social and cognitive learning. The curriculum should include group projects that are investigations of worthwhile topics. They usually include constructions and dramatic play as well as a variety of literacy activities that emerge from the work of the investigation and the tasks of summarising findings and sharing the experiences of the work accomplished.
>
> (Katz 2000)

In *The Literate Classroom,* Lewis (1999) identified a 'five step' approach to the development of writing. However, to consider progression on its own is not enough. We need to contemplate where talk can make a difference to each stage of the writer's development and how we might manage this within the range of learning approaches offered.

Step 1: Immersion in text type
Hearing stories with similar patterns. Partners could work on text familiarisation through challenges and games.

Step 2: Explicit discussion of structure and concrete recording of structure
Whole-class mapping or graphic representation of the story pattern with teacher modelling. Paired talk during shared writing sessions provides thinking time and ideas at word, sentence and text level.

Step 3: Independent recording of the structure
Mapping of further examples of story type. Children engaged in paired writing, working in pairs to add ideas to story 'map', writer/checker roles, planning, deciding on and making individual contributions.

Step 4: Using structure to plan own story
Using own ideas with some kind of planning frame. Children collaborating to review and question against previously agreed criteria.

Step 5: Drafting and reviewing

Sharing the drafts in a plenary. It is possible to work in larger groups with different individual responsibilities. Pairs or groups may review at different stages in an extended piece of writing, questioning against criteria for a good piece of writing, e.g. how the audience may be affected at word, sentence and text level.

QCA guidance (1999) also provides support when planning for writing. The following grid has been developed with reference to the QCA planning guidance. Each one of the suggested activities contains speaking and listening skills that can work to support the understanding and knowledge of different writing genres.

Year 1	• retelling story, adding details in turn • turn taking to record data on a story map or chart • repeating instructions in sequence to support each other • expressing views on how story has been presented • joining in with a partner on repetitions • sequencing activity – events, plot
Year 2	• commenting constructively against story 'criteria' • asking relevant questions of each other • remembering specific points (active listening) • identifying what they know or have learnt • allocating tasks within paired writing • supporting each other's work
Year 3	• identifying main points/features • asking relevant questions to clarify • responding directly to specific points made • agreeing what is known of plot or character
Year 4	• identifying main effects for presentation • making notes • identifying main points of each speaker in constructing and argument • comparing arguments • reviewing progress at intervals
Year 5	• critical review – using open and closed questions to review their own work • sorting fact from opinion • working to time-scales of completion of different stages
Year 6	• offering points of view in constructing large-scale writing projects • note-taking and editing techniques • discussing organisation of paragraphs/points • synthesising ideas and evaluating outcomes

The activities listed in this grid have been grouped according to the QCA framework so that they could become part of a whole-school approach to developing writing to be selected at different stages in a writer's development. However, effective and purposeful talk doesn't just happen. Initially different skills that talk partners can use will need to be directly taught and practised for short bursts of time during a whole-class or group activity. QCA recommends that: 'Given the significance of speaking and listening and language development, it is important to identify adequate curriculum time and to maximise opportunities in existing provision.'

Teachers need to ask questions regarding how all the advice about planning for speaking and listening during writing would work in their classrooms.

- At what stage of development are the children in becoming independent writers within any specific genre of writing?
- What might be possible at this stage in terms of speaking and listening? Is the writing being done in pairs, groups or by an individual? Is the structure of a writing frame needed or should the frame be taken away?
- If working in pairs, will children do so all the way through the writing or will they only work on one part (beginning, middle or end) together? What will be most appropriate for individual children? Will paired writing restrict some but support others?
- What speaking and listening skills might be appropriate to use within the paired or group writing?

Children working as talk and writing partners

How did the children talk to each other as they wrote? The following examples of five- and six-year-olds' conversations show them discussing an ongoing piece of writing. Throughout the process, the questioning and response is full of concerns about 'getting it right', i.e. clarifying spelling conventions and teacher expectation, audience awareness, conventions of presentation, review and suggestions for improvement/ development, making judgements about language and when to use it effectively.

Abby:	How do you spell 'squeezed'?
Sophie:	I don't know, but I know it's got a 'q' sound near the start.
Abby:	Yes, you do that with a 'q' and a 'u' don't you?
Sophie:	Yes.
Jordan:	I'm using that good word 'wreck' in my story. Miss Whitlow might say it's a good word.
Georgina:	Can I read mine for everyone? I think mine is going to be good. I'm just coming to the exciting bit. (She reads the start of her story)
Reece:	Yeah, a good word for you to write next is 'suddenly' 'cos something exciting is going to happen.
Georgina:	And if I do it in capitals it will be even better.
Teacher:	Why is that?
Georgina:	People will think something big is going to happen.
Alannah:	Is the octopus going to get you?
Georgina:	Yes, but I'll get away.

Sometimes we teachers feel if we don't talk, we're not teaching. The truth is teachers can talk too much and interfere. As one colleague said, 'I am much more aware now of providing opportunities for children to speak and listen to each other, as well as an adult'. QCA outlines significant factors that underpin the role of teacher:

- Modelling appropriate speaking and listening, including as a supportive and probing listener.

- Encouraging sensitive interaction.
- Ensuring goals are set with clear criteria for success.

Teacher talk

In Barnwell Primary, as a result of the heightened awareness across the whole school, teachers began to discuss their findings and consider how important the 'process' had been in constructing opportunities to learn. In particular, one teacher had a student working alongside her in the classroom. When the student had tried to copy the strategies for paired talk, the session had not gone well and many children were not involved. The class teacher said: 'On analysis we noted that the children had not been given any thinking time or enough time to talk within their small groups. The student hadn't given any time limits to the children within which to work – dominant children took over, others became uninterested. This made me realise I now take for granted a lot of the strategies and don't explicitly plan for them.' The teacher and student worked together to develop the following strategy list for the next day:

Ensure children are in groups and they know whom they will be talking to.

Ensure children are in a comfortable position for listening, i.e. facing their partner/group.

Pose a problem for discussion.

Allow for a short thinking time.

Allow time for talking and use intervention to ensure all are participating.

Gather ideas and value all contributions.

Allow more time for talking and the gathering of more ideas.

Use the ideas from the children in shared writing.

Keep it pacey, providing short bursts of time for thinking and talking.

Other examples of teacher reflection have focused upon the following changes they felt they had made to their own practice:

Lessons have more structure – children are allowed time to think about what they will need to write.

More planning goes into the activities that precede the writing task.

I plan the questions I will ask and try to use more open questions.

I have a greater awareness of different levels of capability in speaking and listening as well as writing.

I do not expect children to produce an extended piece of writing unless different aspects have been clearly modelled.

I let children 'try out their ideas' with each other.

I have attempted paired writing in addition to producing one piece each.

I encourage children to work in different partnerships, i.e. same/different ability, sex, age.

I work with partnerships across the curriculum.

I now fully believe in the children having knowledge and understanding before they write – without giving them a foundation on which to work is unproductive. They also need time.

Conclusion

As I write, the school is taking time to assess improvements made in writing. Evidence provided through monitoring shows that the structure of children's writing is more sound and it is lexically richer. Presentation is clearer and more appealing to the reader. Children are able to explore a wider range of writing drawn from 'first hand' experience. Forward planning incorporates an extended writing opportunity each week and there is a weekly 'Gold Book' award for a portfolio of accumulated work from each class. It is clear that the school has worked hard to provide their children with valid tickets for the writing journey and clear maps so they don't get lost. As they travel, children are not restricted in their view through the window and are encouraged to explore and talk about the whole range of images that they can see. One of the teachers, Rachel Whitlow, confidently states that: 'Our children seem to be under the writing spell – they love it and are brimming with confidence, even if they are not very able.' Fundamentally, children feel excitement and anticipation as they get ready to step onto the train, and more confident to leap across the gap as they leave the platform.

References

Bereiter, C. and Scardamalia, M. (1987) *The Psychology of Written Composition.* New Jersey: Lawrence Erlbaum.

Katz, L. (2000) 'Another look at what young children should be learning', *National School Improvement Network News* **16**, 5–7.

Lewis, M. (1999) 'Developing children's narrative writing using story structures', in Goodwin, P. (ed.) *The Literate Classroom.* London: David Fulton Publishers.

QCA (1999) *Teaching Speaking and Listening Skills in Key Stages 1 and 2.* London: QCA.

Chapter 8

Sorting out learning through group talk
Sue Lyle

A first grade teacher in America gave her children the first half of a selection of proverbs to complete. In response to one of the proverbs a child wrote:

The pen is mightier than ... *the pig.*

For those of us familiar with the proverb, the idea of considering the 'pen' to be a device for housing pigs appears at first sight to be illogical; as we reflect and see how 'pen' is a word which carries different meanings in different contexts, we readily appreciate the logic of the child who interpreted it in this way. This example serves to remind us that children are persistent and logical thinkers, active meaning makers who struggle to make sense of the world. It was the research of Wells (1985) and Tizzard and Hughes (1984) that alerted us to the intellectual struggle of young children and showed us how sensitive adults, who provide opportunities for children to engage in conversation with others, can make an enormous difference to children's learning and development. Their work encouraged the development of a genuinely communicative agenda between adults and children to promote their cognitive and linguistic development.

Since this early pioneering work, we have learnt a great deal about how classroom processes can enhance children's thinking and learning. The importance of talk to children's learning is now well established and over the last twenty years a substantial body of research has provided us with evidence of how children use talk to learn, and of the classroom practices which can best support such learning (see for example, Norman 1992). This includes the consideration of pupil grouping, the development of ground rules for talk, clear learning outcomes which are shared with the children, and the selection of suitable topics for discussion (for a review of the literature on children's collaborative talk see Lyle 1997). Most recently, the influence of Vygotskyan approaches to learning have focused on the potential repertoire of roles the teacher could adopt in the learning process, with an emphasis on appropriate and effective intervention.

More recently, our ideas about how children learn are supported by the latest research on the neurological function of the brain that has made us much more aware of the effect our classroom practices have on its development. Smith (1996) summarises some of this research as follows:

- A new learning experience needs to be located on, or connected to, existing pathways for meaning to be generated.
- For the brain to validate learning there has to be an emotional connection.
- Humans can never really understand something until they can create a personal metaphor or model.

It would seem that evidence from classrooms and research on the brain tells us that learning or making meaning is shaped by a culture's toolkit and ways of thought. This way of thinking about learning has come to be known as the *socio-cultural model.*

The socio-cultural model

The socio-cultural model is concerned with the ways in which understanding develops. America's leading educational psychologist, Jerome Bruner talks of two distinct ways of making sense of the world: the *logico-mathematical* and *narrative understanding* (Bruner 1996). Of these two he regards narrative as a universal way of making sense, of ordering experiences used by all cultures. Bruner (1990, p. 80) suggests that there is some human 'readiness' or predisposition to organise experience into narrative form – that human beings have an 'innate' and primitive predisposition to narrative organisation, regardless of culture or age or preferred styles of learning. In fact work within different disciplinary areas shows that narrative understanding may well be *the* major, cognitive tool through which human beings make sense of the world (for a summary of this position see Lyle 2000). This has profound implications for how we present the curriculum and how we structure learning experiences for children.

By examining the features of narrative we may find some clues to help us use the concept of narrative understanding to construct classroom activities. If we turn to our earliest story forms, the classic folk-tales, we find binary opposites form the most prominent structuring elements in such narratives: good/evil; bravery/cowardice; fear/security; hope/despair and so on. In his research on fables and fairy tales Bettelheim (1976, p. 74) points out that: 'the manner in which the child can bring some order into his world is by dividing everything into opposites'.

Can we learn anything from this? Egan (1991) says we can. He suggests that the use of binary opposites is in fact a fundamental way in which human beings make sense of the world which can be harnessed by teachers to help organise learning experiences for children; in fact, classification is fundamental to almost all human activity. We all use organising principles all the time to make sense of our world; a trip to the supermarket is enough to convince us of the importance of categorisation, without the order imposed by the layout of the supermarket, our shopping trips would be chaotic.

In this chapter I use extracts from children's talk to show how the use of binary opposites and rules of classification can promote effective learning through collaborative talk. At the same time, I suggest that learning strategies which enable children to handle information effectively are of immense importance as we enter the 'information age'. Many commentators have recently pointed out that one of our biggest challenges is learning how to deal with information overload. In the future it is not knowing things, but how to manage information that will be valued. Perhaps one of our oldest ways of organising information can be employed to help children make sense of today's world. Binary opposites form the basis of classification, a major tool through which we can organise information and mediate understanding. Furthermore, binary opposites and classification are powerful cognitive tools we can harness to help plan classroom activities and help children develop the kind of categorical thinking associated with cognitive development.

Card sorting activities

One way in which teachers can apply these concepts is by devising card sorting activities which set up binary opposites for children to mediate. As participants read information on cards for the purpose of sorting them into different categories or classifications, they can learn about people, places and issues in ways which are meaningful, by drawing on existing knowledge to generate new understanding. In this way new learning can be connected to 'existing pathways' to build and generate meaning (Smith 1996).

When card sorting activities are organised for children in collaborative groups they have the opportunity to negotiate meaning as they interrogate the information on the cards. In the following example, four boys are following an activity from *A Rainforest Child* (Lyle and Roberts 1986, 3rd edn 1992). Having shuffled and dealt the cards out between them, the task is to take it in turns to read a card and together decide how to place each card according to predetermined criteria. This provides the catalyst for discussion and exchange of ideas. In the first extract that follows, the children have to sort the cards into two piles: information about how people who live in the rainforest use the forest, and information about how people who do not live in the forest use it (for a full discussion of this activity see Lyle 1993). The extract begins with John reading one of the cards to the others.

Extract 1

John:	*In the many rivers and streams there are thousands of different fish to catch and eat.*
Steffan:	That would be rain ...
John:	(interrupting) that could be both (rainforest people and us) as well.
Owen:	But normally it would be them.
James:	You don't really see that many tropical fish in our shops do you?
Owen:	(nodding) That would be them (rainforest people).
James:	We just have mackerel.
John:	That would definitely be them, because we eat stuff from our rivers and ...
Owen:	Seas as well ...
John:	... and we do eat fish from seas abroad ... but ... we don't do it very much in the tropics do we?
Owen:	The fish would go bad really.
James:	The fish would go bad as well ... wouldn't it?
Steffan:	We usually get our fish from the sea don't we, not from the river.
Owen:	Both.

Throughout this section of talk the children work together to establish meaning. In doing so they draw on their own knowledge of the world to help them interpret the information. Through discussion children find new patterns for what is already known and apply these patterns to other situations. In this example, binary opposites provide a structured way of organising information; it is a cultural tool which can be harnessed to mediate children's talk and can stimulate discussion and debate.

The next extract from the rainforest card sorting activity comes near the beginning of the task when the boys have not yet gained the confidence to make decisions about some of the cards. This time it is Steffan's turn to begin.

Extract 2

Steffan:	*Lots of things which are good to eat like mushrooms and berries grow wild in the rainforest.*

James:	That's them.
Steffan:	(agreeing) That's them isn't it?
James:	'Cos ... um ...
John:	Wait, we eat ... we eat tropical fruit more than they do.
Steffan:	Yeah, we do, don't we? (questioning tone)
John:	We eat bananas, oranges.
James:	I'm not sure on that now ... put it in the middle.

Here the boys are tentative, after first agreeing that the card describes how they (rain-forest people) use the forest they realise they haven't got any evidence to support their judgement (James: 'Cos ... um). John's comment is enough to make both Steffan and James unsure, and they decide to come back to the card later. When they do come back to it they have built criteria for decision making and provide reasoned arguments for placing the card on the rainforest pile.

In collaborative card sorting activities, the meanings children make are not stable, but fluid and changing, built up from their existing knowledge, the information on the cards, and their negotiated decision making. Meanings change and develop in response to discussion and lead to a gradually more sophisticated interrogation and interpretation of the cards over time.

The next set of extracts comes from a student teacher who made an audio recording of a group of children engaged in a classification exercise. They were asked to sort rainforest animals according to whether they were mammals, reptiles, birds, fish or invertebrates. The instruction sheet contains information about each animal's characteristics and the children are told they should back up their decisions about where to place each card from their reading. In the first extract the children begin to use the classification criteria, but do not feel confident enough to make up their minds and decide to come back to the card later.

Extract 3

Andrew:	(reading the card) *Armadillo. They eat a wide variety of food from the forest floor, insects, snakes, small mammals and plants. The young are born with a leathery skin which hardens to form the armadillo's armoured back.* It has leathery skin so it hasn't got any fur.
Nia:	It doesn't look like a reptile or invertebrate.
Gareth:	I can't decide, shall we leave it until last and have another think about it?

In the next discussion, the correct classification is obvious from the card, it is clearly 'a fish', but note how the children use the classificatory information before placing the card on the correct pile.

Extract 4

Jenna:	*Lungfish. This fish has paired lungs and only small gills. When the Amazon streams in which it lives dry out it burrows in the mud and breathes air.*
Gareth:	It says 'this fish'...
Andrew:	It's got gills.
Nia:	It burrows in the mud.
Andrew:	Well, it lives in water.
Gareth:	I said it was a fish.

In Extract 5, the children are using the classificatory criteria with confidence, but Jenna seems to doubt a manatee is a mammal. Andrew, who draws on his knowledge of whales to provide an answer to Jenna's problem, answers her query; Gareth also provides evidence to support Andrew. This gives Jenna confidence to signal her agreement with the others by referring to the criteria. By the end of the sequence the children show how they can use their knowledge of the world and the evidence on the cards to make their decision.

Extract 5

Nia:	*Manatee. They live in the larger rivers in the forest, swimming with their paddle-like flippers. They feed on water plants. A manatee calf is born in the water and is fed on milk by its mother.*
Andrew:	If it's fed on milk it's born a mammal.
Jenna:	But it hasn't got any hair.
Gareth:	It probably has but you can't really see it.
Andrew:	Some whales are mammals.
Jenna:	Yes, and for mammals it says they suckle their young so it must be a mammal.
Nia:	Yes, I think it must be a mammal.

Finally, in the last extract the children return to their discussion of the armadillo. By this stage the children are much more confident and demonstrate their understanding of the classificatory system for organising information about animals. To help them decide into which category an animal should be placed they refer to what an animal is not, as well as what it is. They ask questions to help restrict the description to one classification.

Extract 6

Gareth:	*Armadillo. They eat a wide variety of food from the forest floor, insects, snakes, small mammals and plants. The young are born with a leathery skin which hardens to form the armadillo's armoured back.* Doesn't look like a reptile …
Andrew:	… got a backbone.
Nia:	It is probably a mammal.
Jenna:	It's not an invertebrate.
Andrew:	Does the card say anything about the young?
Gareth:	Yes, it says …
Andrew:	Yes it says about young being born so it's a mammal.

These extracts demonstrate the importance of the dialogue the children engage in. Through talk, or what Bakhtin (1981) has called 'dialogic engagement', participants in collaborative card sorting activities can be enabled to jointly construct understanding. The involvement of children as both speakers and listeners means speakers contribute, respond, build and modify their ideas to create meaning over stretches of discourse. It is also important to remember that the linguistic behaviour of each child in a group activity will reflect past social experiences within the social group, and not merely be a 'window' into what a child knows or is thinking. In Extract 1, Owen, a low-achieving child, contributes well to the conversation on fish, reflecting his personal knowledge: his father regularly takes him both river and sea fishing. He is making a 'personal, emotional connection' (Smith 1996) which will help his learning. Andrew (Extract 5) clearly knows that whales are mammals and is able to use that information to make inferences about manatees. If intersubjectivity (Portecorvo 1997) is to be achieved, there must be a full sharing of activity and discourse between the participants. Ensuring this happens is not easy, but is assisted by carefully structured tasks which allocate turns and require debate and discussion.

When children work successfully in collaborative groups, the access to each other's experience and knowledge allows them to make productive connections. As views are shared there is the potential for change or extension of current understanding. Children who have different understandings or interpretations of the tasks can negotiate meaning through talk. Such talk is more easily generated by some tasks than others, and it is important that teachers select suitable topics for talk treatment.

Interpreting visual images

The power of classification as a learning tool is highlighted in the next example of children's talk. In a project involving 21 student teachers and three classes of Year 5 (age 10) children, data was collected in the form of student field notes and extracts from children's talk as they studied *A River Child* (Lyle and Hendley 1992). In this extract children examine a culturegram – a poster of photographic and illustrated images of a village in Nigeria – and generate ideas about the people and place. The children were asked to brainstorm their ideas under four headings: work, leisure, environment and way of life. This strategy helps the children make sense of the visual images. The student teachers observed the children in their discussions and made notes of their exchanges. The following extracts have been taken from the students' notes. The poster contains images of fishing and in the following exchange the children are trying to decide whether this is evidence of work or leisure:

Marc:	Fishing is a sport.
Nia:	If people don't like fish they wouldn't have much food to eat.
Katie:	Fishing is how they get food, so it's work.
Marc:	Fishing is for fun.
Nia:	Yeah, but not in this picture.
Simon:	So it's work.
Marc:	OK.

Here we see children qualifying or justifying what they think after listening to the thoughts and opinions of others. Comparing and contrasting and looking for similarities and differences between their own lives and the lives of people in the village were important strategies used by the children to make meaning as notes by many of the students suggest: for example, 'The children compared their own daily routines and lives to the activities they could see in the poster to help establish meaning'.

In the next example the children have decided to discuss the health of the people. Initially the children had assumed that because the poster depicted a village in Africa that the people would not be healthy; their own stereotyped images of Africa had mediated their interpretation of the images. The student teacher challenged this and asked the children to look more carefully at the poster. In the next extract Amy challenges the group's initial assumption that people in Africa are not healthy by pointing to evidence in the poster. Katy supports Amy, and Darren takes it further, drawing on his implicit understanding of his own cultural world and using that to speculate on the unfamiliar:

Amy: The people are healthy because they've got good, strong, white teeth.
Katy: That comes from eating the fish they catch and fresh produce they grow.
Darren: Everything's fresh really, it wouldn't be tinned or come out of a packet.

When children are asked to respond to visual images teachers often ask them to brainstorm their ideas. In this example the children were given categories to help organise their thinking. By asking them to cluster their ideas according to headings they start to search out meaning and impose structure on their brainstorming. In order for learning to be meaningful we all have to organise new experiences according to how we can relate to them and compare them with what we already know and think. I would suggest that classification and categorisation are the cornerstones of meaningful learning.

Interpreting graphical data

In the final example, children are involved in comparing contrasting climates – Britain and the Arctic – by looking at graphical data in the form of temperature graphs. In this task the children use binary opposites to discriminate features of the environment and use their ideas to speculate how such features would affect the lives of the people who live in these places. The graphs provide a highly contextualised activity for the children's discussion. The children are told to organise their discussion by generating headings which help to structure their talk. In this extract the children discuss what those headings should be:

James: It (temperatures) will affect their housing.
John: Yeah and clothes.
Steffan: (questioning tone) Housing, clothes, um … animals?
Ben: (affirming) Animals.
James: Food, plants – animals and foods.
Steffan: Mmm.
John: What else … entertainment?
Steffan: No.
Ben: Leisure.
Steffan: Yeah, leisure.
James: John (scribe for the group), have you written them all down?

The boys have chosen headings for discussion and systematically discuss each heading in turn. The headings break down a complex task and render it more manageable. This, in turn, structured their subsequent talk in a particular way as they worked through their own headings and recorded their observations. Notice how they use knowledge of their own world as a springboard into the unknown. They start with 'housing' and begin by speculating about the heating required:

James: Housing. It would have to be a lot warmer than most houses – they
            wouldn't have any central heating would they – just a wood fire.
Steffan: Yes they'd have fires.
James: (laughing) Lots of them I'd expect.
Steffan: Yes, but where would … it would be hard to find the wood.
James: Yes, wood … well they don't have to burn wood, they could have any
            other fuel.
Ben: Burn ice.
John: Yeah, they might.
James   No, I don't think so.

The boys are silent for a short while before returning to the topic of housing.

Ben:	Houses ... they wouldn't be able to make them out of brick.
James:	No, they'd probably make it out of mud.
John:	No, they'd make it out of ... IGLOOS!
James:	Oh, ice ... how come when they make a fire it doesn't melt the igloo?
Steffan:	Some houses in the Arctic are made out of ... wood and bricks, they are honestly.
Ben:	Yeah, I know, I saw it on 'White Fang'.
Steffan:	Yeah, so did I.
James:	I went to see that, it's good. ... They would have ice houses, but *now* they have wood.

Later on the boys consider each of the headings and make a number of tentative suggestions which indicate they are using evidence from the graphs to inform their speculations. All the extracts show children working in the hypothetical mode (see italics). Here John is discussing clothes:

John:	Their clothes would *have to be* made of animal skins.

Later James and then Steffan reflect on the animals:

James:	They would *have to be* um ... carnivores.
Steffan:	The animals would *have to be* good at hunting.

In small collaborative groups children get the opportunity to ask questions to clarify their thinking. Later, when discussing food, Steffan asks a question which John is able to answer:

Steffan:	What's food got to do with the weather?
James:	I don't know.
John:	Well, it would mean that only certain things could live there and only certain plants could grow there.

These extracts show that the use of focus materials such as graphs to generate discussion based on binary opposites and classification can promote purposeful linguistic interaction between children. Activities of this kind provide a context for learning in which children can make meaning out of the graphical data in front of them. The boys drew on the meaning structures and experiences they already possessed and combined this with their ability to imagine what kind of world might exist in very different temperatures. They used concrete knowledge of their own climate to mediate an understanding of the very cold. Through making comparisons and looking for similarities and differences the children are able to form concepts and identify relationships between them (for a full discussion of this activity see Lyle 1998).

Conclusion

In each of the above examples children use binary opposites as a cognitive tool as they struggle to make sense of classroom tasks. The mediation of binary opposites provides a focus which sustains children's dialogues as they discuss different viewpoints. The materials discussed here are taken from teaching packs which have an overall narrative structure and make use of binary opposites and classificatory processes to stimulate learners' understanding of themselves as well as others. The activities allow the children to relate information to their existing understanding of the world. They use this knowledge to interpret information and in the process reshape or redefine it. Binary opposites provide different ways of looking at phenomena, it is therefore a cultural tool which can be harnessed to mediate children's discussion.

In each of these extracts the children put forward ideas, provide reasons for their thinking, use the hypothetical mode when they are unsure, take up and build on one another's points. When they make decisions they seek to justify them with evidence. The centrality of speaking and listening to these activities is clear. Through discussion of graphs, information on cards, or visual images, children were engaging with text; it was the talk which enabled them to engage with the content, and through interaction with each other, make productive connections. It is this social experience which affects the course of individual development which links to Vygotsky's socio-cultural model of learning which moves external and social acts to internal and mental acts.

It is now widely accepted that opportunities need to be found for children to engage in collaborative talk to establish meaning. If binary opposites and classification are to be taken seriously as tools for structuring such classroom processes then teachers need to look for opportunities in the National Curriculum to do so. In this chapter the subjects of geography and science have been drawn on to provide examples of activities: in fact all subjects of the curriculum can draw on these cognitive tools to help children learn.

References

Bahktin, M. M. (1981) *The Dialogic Imagination: Four Essays by M. M. Bakhtin*, ed. Holquist, M., trans. Emerson, C. and Holquist, M. Austin: University of Texas Press.

Bettelheim, B. (1976) *The Uses of Enchantment: the meaning and importance of fairy tales*. London: Penguin.

Bruner, J. (1990) *Acts of meaning*. Cambridge, Mass.: Harvard University Press.

Bruner, J. (1996) *The culture of education*. Cambridge, Mass.: Harvard University Press.

Egan, K. (1991) *Primary Understanding: education in early childhood*. New York: Routledge.

Lyle, S. (1993) 'An investigation into ways in which children "Talk themselves into meaning"', *Language and Education* **7**(3), 181–98.

Lyle, S. (1997) 'Children's collaborative talk', in Davies, B. (ed) *Encyclopaedia of Language and Education Vol. 3: Oral Discourse and Education*, 197–206. Dordrecht, Netherlands: Kluwer.

Lyle, S. (1998) 'Collaborative talk and meaning making in primary classrooms', Doctoral Dissertation, University of Reading.

Lyle, S. (2000) 'Narrative understanding: developing a theoretical context for understanding how children make meaning in classroom settings', *Journal of Curriculum Studies* **32**(1), 45–63.

Lyle, S. and Hendley, D. (1992) *A River Child*. Swansea: Swansea Institute of Higher Education.

Lyle, S. and Roberts, M. (1986) *A Rainforest Child*, 3rd edn 1992. Carmarthen: Greenlight Publications.

Norman, K. (ed.) (1992) *Thinking Voices: The work of the National Oracy Project*. Sevenoaks: Hodder & Stoughton.

Portecorvo, D. (1997) 'Classroom discourse for the making of learning', in Davies, B. (ed.) *Encyclopaedia of Language and Education Vol. 3: Oral Discourse and Education*, 169–78. Dordrecht, Netherlands: Kluwer

Smith, A. (1996) *Accelerated Learning*. Stafford: Network Educational Press Ltd.

Tizard, B. and Hughes, M. (1984) *Young children learning, talking, and thinking at home and at school in the inner city*. Brighton: Lawrence Erlbaum.

Wells, G. (1985) *Language development in the pre-school years*. Cambridge: Cambridge University Press.

Chapter 9

'Five little dollies jumping on the bed' – Learning about mathematics through talk
Janet Evans

> On Monday in maths class, Mrs Fibonacci says, 'You know, you can think of almost everything as a maths problem.' On Tuesday I started having problems. ... The whole morning is one problem after another. ... There are 24 kids in my class. Jake scratches his paper with one finger. How many fingers are in our class? Casey pulls Eric's ear. How many ears are in our class? The new girl, Kelly, sticks her tongue out at me. How many tongues in our class? I'm about to really lose it, when the lunch bell rings.
>
> (Scieszka 1995[1])

The anguished character in Jon Scieszka's book, *Maths Curse*, feels as though she has had a curse placed upon her. She is a brilliant mathematician for her age (probably about seven- or eight-years-old) but the more she tries not to think about maths problems in her daily life the more they appear, and the more her mathematical brain works overtime. She is working all by herself with her very inventive imagination. Her teacher, Mrs Fibonacci, isn't giving her any practical help with the problems, let alone talking to her about them. In fact, there is no one for her to talk to as she struggles to solve the number problems. No wonder she feels she is turning into a maths raving lunatic. After a stressful period of time, the young genius manages to solve her mathematical problems. She is not free of stress, however, as the original problems are replaced straightaway by another set, this time related to science, and the whole cycle starts again.

Despite nearly going crazy, the young character in the fictional *Maths Curse* manages to solve her problems alone. However, most children need a bit more support and, by providing the chance to talk in a supportive, non-threatening environment, they can articulate their experiences, which helps them to make sense of what is being considered. The ability to think, problem solve, apply problems to real situations and to talk about these situations are some of the characteristics of good mathematicians. Do these skills and abilities come naturally or do they need nurturing and teaching?

This chapter looks at why talk is important for young children as they learn about mathematics. It considers how talk fosters mathematical understanding and the importance of having something to talk about which relates maths to real situations. It then describes some four- and five-year-old children talking about simple number activities linked to a favourite rhyming story-song, highlighting their revealing comments on different mathematical ideas.

---

[1] From MATH CURSE by Jon Scieszka, copyright © 1995 Jon Scieszka. Used by permission of Viking Penguin, an imprint of Penguin Putnam Books for Young Readers, a division of Penguin Putnam Inc.

Talk is important

Much work done during the period of the National Oracy Project (1987–93) focused on the way in which children learn through talk. Gordon Wells (1992), who was asked to review some of the articles representing the work of the Oracy Project, was clearly delighted to be able to say that, 'the centrality of talk in education is finally being recognised'. The centrality of talk was evident in the work that some teachers were doing with early years children (Norman 1990). The teachers listened to children and, in some instances, were surprised that the youngsters could sustain purposeful talk for lengthy periods of time when they were engaged in meaningful activities. The teachers saw how the children's talk provided real evidence of their learning and they noticed that, if the activity was meaningful, the talk and subsequent learning would flow naturally. Current developments in early years education are stressing the important role of the educator for promoting learning through talk whilst at the same time moving towards increasing independence for children. The Qualifications and Curriculum Authority's *Curriculum Guidance for the Foundation Stage* (QCA 2000) places speaking and listening in a prominent position by stating in relation to learning in the section on communication, language and literacy that:

> The development and use of communication and language is at the heart of young children's learning. ... In play, children are given the chance to imagine and to recreate experience. ... Young children's learning is not compartmentalised. They learn when they make connections between experiences and ideas that are related to any aspect of their life in the setting, at home and in the community (p. 45).

In relation to teaching, in this same section QCA state:

> Children will become confident speakers if talk is valued in the setting and they are encouraged to want to communicate. ... Children will learn to understand and be aware of other points of view if practitioners demonstrate strategies such as listening, turn taking and initiating and sustaining a conversation gently and respectfully. ... Children learn to use language in its immediate context first (p. 46).

The prominence given to talk in the new curriculum guidance for the early years shows just how important it is. Children learn through talking about things that are meaningful and relevant to them and their oral language reflects their current understandings of what is being considered. The new curriculum documentation also places play in a more central position than has recently been the case and the links between play, talk and learning are clear.

Different kinds of maths talk

It is important to plan for and provide activities that will promote mathematical talk and hopefully lead on to mathematical learning. However, not all kinds of talk promote learning and, as The Mathematical Association, in a book entitled *Maths Talk* (1987) points out, 'The lessons in which the teacher is the "talker", while the children are silent or monosyllabic, are not suitable for the development of mathematical language' (p. 21). *Maths Talk* highlights three different types of 'mathematics talk': talk that is teacher led, child–teacher talk, and talk between the children themselves. These three types of mathematics talk all have important parts to play in the various stages of the National Numeracy Strategy (NNS) numeracy hour (DfEE 1999). In the first type the teacher is likely to be introducing and explaining new skills and concepts to the children, in the second the teacher may be asking questions and inviting discussion. It is in the third type, where children are encouraged to talk amongst themselves, that much learning often takes place through focused, on task discussion.

In his book on talking and learning in mathematics, Ball (1990) was concerned by the kinds of questions which were often asked in child–teacher talk. True discussion requires group members to work collaboratively, take turns, express ideas, be prepared to argue a point logically, and, give and accept constructive criticism. It is clear that discussion is a skill in itself which children need to learn. If teachers only ask closed questions requiring yes/no or right/wrong answers then the skills of discussion will not be nurtured. By asking open questions we invite children to think about what is being considered. Chambers (1993) argues that to get the best kind of responses from children teachers should not be asking questions all the time but should be inviting them to tell us what they think. By introducing more talk into our mathematics teaching there are benefits to be had which are not all confined to learning about maths. Ball (1990) believes that discussion:

- improves language skills;
- develops understanding;
- encourages positive attitudes;
- promotes social and personal skills;

all of which contribute to successful learning, no matter what the subject being studied.

Something to talk about

To learn about mathematics through talk one must have something to talk about. The talk of young children is more likely to lead to purposeful learning if it is related to practical activities presented in the form of play experiences. The Mathematical Association looked at the relationship between experience, language and learning. They acknowledged that from a very early age children's activities form the basis of much language exchange. It is the experience that generates the language and leads on to learning: Experience ➜ Language ➜ Learning (*Maths Talk*, 1987).

Unfortunately, some children are still taught mathematics in a manner which does not emphasise understanding. They can be seen working in silence on pages of meaningless sums that do not relate to real experiences in their everyday life. To be relevant, mathematics skills need to be applied to particular situations; children must be able to recognise which skills are relevant, then be able to apply them. This means that teachers need to present mathematics to young children in ways which are as near to real life situations as possible and which take into consideration the ways in which children learn.

Teaching mathematics to young children

Educators have always been concerned with the ways in which children learn and develop. From the 1920s onwards, educators and academic researchers such as Piaget, Vygotsky and Bruner have carried out research into young children's learning. They suggest that young children need to understand things in their own ways through being actively involved with their environment, through talk and social interaction and through being provided with relevant, meaningful situations to which they could relate. The notion of presenting children with learning situations which are of immediate relevance is implicit in Bruner's proposition that learning takes place recursively, starting at a simple level conceptually, spiralling forward and gradually building up to quite complex concepts (Bruner 1966). Three phases can be used to represent the way in which learners learn new ideas and can be used to plan for the teaching and learning of new concepts in the young child's classroom environment.

- Enactive: a practical, concrete, 'doing' phase.
- Iconic: a pictorial phase where pictures, diagrams and sketches replace the concrete 'doing' phase.
- Symbolic: an abstract stage where abstract symbols both written and spoken replace the other phases.

In the first, enactive, 'doing' phase, children are involved with practical experiences, for example playing in the sand, role play in the home corner, baking, modelling, dressing up, playing with masks, puppets and soft toys. The *experience–language–learning* formula can be used to describe exactly what is happening in these situations where children are playing individually, in pairs and in larger groups. The children's learning is essentially characterised by real objects, concrete play and oral language. Sometimes structured apparatus made from soft toys can replace the children themselves; this is starting to move the children on to the next phase.

In the second, iconic phase, children are still playing in meaningful situations; however, pictures and diagrams – used for games, sorting, sequencing and matching activities – replace the concrete objects and experiences. The pictures form a bridge, or transition stage, for children who are not quite ready to jump straight into abstract thought processes from the concrete 'doing' phase. Children's learning in this phase is predominantly characterised by representative play (where the pictures represent the real objects) and oral language.

It is in the third, symbolic phase that the previous two phases, both characterised by practical activities, are gradually replaced by abstract thought processes. An ability to think symbolically is not necessarily linked to age but is likely to be a feature of more mature learners. Even adults, when faced with learning something new, often go through the first two stages – enactive and iconic – before reaching the symbolic stage, the point at which they can understand without needing to refer to practical activity or representation.

The three parts of the learning continuum mentioned above are recursive. Children require plenty of time to experience and revisit each stage. The need to move in and out of the enactive, iconic and symbolic stages means that young children must have many concrete experiences before they can internalise ideas and concepts in order to deal with them in an abstract way. Given the centrality of children's talking about their learning to their learning experiences, a suggested format for teaching any new mathematical concept could involve:

- practical work and discussion with children actively involved; for example, with the children physically taking part, the teacher could make a set of children with long hair, with a subset of children with blond long hair;
- substitute concrete materials in place of the children; for example, instead of using the children themselves, make a set of brown shoes or a set of pencil cases;
- apparatus to help children with their own ideas; for example, a set of the children's own teddies;
- purpose made apparatus which emphasises certain attributes and thereby reinforces certain concepts; for example, a set of teddies in four different colours and two sizes;

- a pictorial, intermediate stage using pictures of specific objects. For example, pictures of a set of teddies in four different colours, two sizes and with or without bows.

As the children take part in these activities, different kinds of recording should be ongoing at all times. For example children may make temporary recordings of their sets using any available materials (teachers may like to photograph these if a permanent record is required), and make permanent records such as drawings of their sets of teddies (Evans 1995).

The pattern of learning described above was evident while I was working with some four- and five-year-old children. We had read *Five Ugly Monsters* by Tedd Arnold (1988). *Five Ugly Monsters* is a story-song, which children enjoy, with rhyme and repetition which encourage children to join in – especially with role play. This group of children decided to act out the song but changed the characters to dollies instead of monsters (they had been sorting some dollies for different attributes). During a shared writing session, a slightly different story was made up and written down. This provided a version of the story-song for the children to read together as they acted it out. The new version was:

> *Five little dollies jumping on the bed,*
> *One fell off and bumped its head.*
> *One called for the doctor and the doctor said,*
> *'No more dollies jumping on the bed.'*
>
> *Four little dollies jumping on the bed*
> *(repeat refrain until there are no dollies on the bed)*

To act out the drama, five children were chosen as dollies, one child was a doctor – complete with stethoscope, and one was a narrator. An old pillow was found to jump on. The children proceeded to sing the song and act it out at the same time. They sang and acted, sang and acted and – as the children got to know the words really well – they started to count the dollies. Each time a dolly fell off the bed, the children stopped and I asked one of them to count the dollies still on the bed and those on the floor. Gradually, after many renditions of the song, they were able to see that whenever one dolly fell to the floor there was one less dolly on the bed. They also saw that at the end of the story-song the same number of dollies finished up on the floor as had started on the bed. They had found a pattern and were doing subtraction in an extremely practical and enjoyable manner.

The next stage in the process was for the children to use knitted dollies (structured apparatus) to re-enact the story. The dollies were all dressed in different coloured clothes (see Figure 9.1) and the children held them as they played out the song which, again, was repeated several times.

At this point, the children and I decided to record our counting. We used a skipping rope and made an empty set ring (Venn diagram) on the carpeted area in class. The children all sat around in a circle and we placed the set of *Five Little Dollies* on the bed inside the set ring. We then sang the song again but this time I scribed the number bonds which represented the dollies at each stage in the song. The first part of the story with five dollies jumping on the bed and no dollies on the floor became 5 and 0 = 5. Then four dollies jumping on the bed and one dolly on the floor was written as 4 and 1 = 5. This format continued with the children verbalising the number bonds with the support of the structured apparatus – the dollies. I was acting as support scribe and, with the

Figure 9.1 Photogragh of five little dollies

help of the children, I recorded the number bonds for all to share. We had soon writ-ten the addition number bonds for number five and the children had drawn the dollies themselves to make a set of five little dollies (see Figure 9.2).

Figure 9.2 Children's drawing of five little dollies

I asked the children if they could see anything they would like to comment on in relation to the number bonds recorded in large format. It was interesting to note that quite a few children – out of the Reception class of 30 – had observations to make. I was determined to ensure that their ideas did not turn into a teacher-led question and answer session and I made a conscious effort to join in with the children, as far as possible making comments to keep the flow of conversation going. Kate had the first comment to make:

Kate:	I can see a pattern five, five, five, five, five. Lots of fives.
Sarah:	(quickly following Kate's observation) There's always five at the end, always five dollies.
Niall:	(pointing to the first row of numbers) You just say five, four, three, two, one, nought. You count down.
Alice:	(in response to Niall and pointing to the same row of numbers) The five keeps going littler. It keeps going younger and younger and younger.
Teacher:	What do you mean younger and younger and younger?
Alice:	Five is an older number and 4 is a younger number.
Niall:	Well, one is a little number and two is a bit bigger and three is a bit bigger.
Daniel :	Three is on top of two and one is underneath two.
Teacher:	Gosh, Daniel! I hadn't thought of that. Can anybody see any other patterns?
Daniel:	Five is bigger than four, five is near to four and four is near to three.
Ashleigh:	(referring to other numbers not part of the number sequence) Six is next to five and six is next to seven and seven is next to six.
Teacher:	Wow! That is brilliant. Can anyone else see any other patterns?
Kate:	Four is in a square shape, (she makes a square with her fingers) but five can be any shape or with one in the middle.
Teacher:	What do you mean five can be any shape or with one in the middle?

(Kate did five dots in a row with her fingers, then did four dots in a square shape with a dot in the middle. Other children had comments to make.)

Alice:	Five is one more bigger than four. The five is more bigger than the other numbers.

Their comments were fascinating. They presented me with windows into the minds of these young mathematicians and allowed me to determine where they were up to in terms of their developing mathematical competencies. I had been unsure of whether they would openly share their ideas, however they did and many of their viewpoints displayed insight, were thought provoking and very revealing for four- and five-year-olds. Some of their comments were linked to their concepts of age, showing how they were relating their own experiences of birthdays and growing older with the number patterns (e.g. five as an older number and four as a younger number). Other comments used comparisons that demonstrated that their thinking linked with previous experiences: size (e.g. Alice: 'The five keeps going littler.'), position (e.g. Daniel: 'Three is on top of two and one is underneath two.') and shape (e.g. Kate: 'Four is in a square shape.'). Some children showed that they were able to think in abstractions: for example, when Ashleigh talked about numbers which had not been dealt with in our story-song.

The children's oral contributions, initiated by the stimulus of acting out the story-song and developed by using the practical structured apparatus (the form of knitted dollies) led on to the shared recording between children and teacher. The children had been involved in a variety of activities including listening to, and joining in with, a simple story-song; acting out a story using role play, and sharing the reading of the story. In terms of mathematics, the children had used the language of sorting and sets in context, e.g. a set ring, sets and subsets of dollies, how many, how many altogether. This language led them on to counting from nought to five, doing subtraction from five and addition to five. They also started to investigate mathematical patterns and to use language to express their thoughts and ideas related to number values.

Throughout the whole activity these young children had talked purposefully about their learning, offering points of view about something that was relevant and meaningful to them, joining in role play and discussing with each other and their teacher. It was evident from their responses that through playing, talking and reflecting on their activities they had gained in mathematical awareness and understanding.

References

Arnold, T. (1988) *Five Ugly Monsters*. London: Scholastic Children's Books.

Ball, G. (1990) *Talking and Learning: Primary Maths for the National Curriculum*. Oxford: Blackwell.

Bruner, J. S. (1966) *Towards a Theory of Instruction*. Harvard: Harvard University Press.

Chambers, A. (1993) *Tell Me: Children, Reading and Talk*. Stroud: The Thimble Press.

DfEE (1999) *The National Numeracy Strategy: Framework for Teaching Mathematics from Reception to Year 6*. London: DfEE.

Evans, J. (1995) *Have Some Maths with Your Story*. Liverpool: Janev Publications.

Scieszka, J. and Smith, L. (1995) *Maths Curse*. Harmondsworth: Viking.

Norman, K. (1990) 'About the Oracy Project', *Child Education*, July, 22–3.

QCA (2000) *Curriculum Guidance for the Foundation Stage*. London: QCA.

The Mathematical Association (1987) *Maths Talk*. Cheltenham: Stanley Thornes.

Wells, G. (1992) 'The centrality of talk in education', in Norman, K. (ed.) *Thinking Voices: the work of the National Oracy Project*, 283–91. Sevenoaks: Hodder and Stoughton.

Chapter 10

IT's all talk?
Frank Monaghan

Information Technology (IT) has gained such a pervasive and dominant position in discussions about education and literacy that it has now begun to attract its very own backlash. Sven Birkerts' apocalyptic vision of the fate of reading in an electronic age in *The Gutenberg Elegies* for instance, was an early entrant into the field in 1994. This is no bad thing, perhaps. As with other technological innovations that promised to radically transform the nature of teaching and learning and didn't (radio, television, laser discs, Prestel, etc.), the computer has begun to find a more realistic identity and role among teachers. It is now perceived as a useful (if sometimes frustrating) tool that works best when integrated into the 'ordinary' practice of the classroom – an extension *to* not a substitute *for* good teaching practices. Lachs (2000) provides some excellent examples of this.

That said, many teachers still remain wary of the machine in the corner and have doubts about their own abilities to use it, let alone to scaffold their pupils' use of it. This is especially true of the kind of software under discussion here, bilingual multimedia software, which requires the teacher to marshal not only text in two languages but also sound recordings and images. It is a commonplace assumption that children are the real IT experts and generally know more than their teachers about computers. While this is not often the case in practice, it is not unusual for children to be left to work largely unsupervised at the computer. This may sometimes be entirely appropriate – as Tony Edwards (1992, p. 240) points out, 'on some occasions, the teacher's best contribution may be not to be there at all'. Knowing when not to intervene is at least as difficult as knowing when to do so and the computer has now added a further complicating variable to that equation. The work that is done at the computer cannot be adequately assessed on the basis of a print-out at the end of the session. Nor is it usefully seen as somehow separate from everything else that goes on both at and away from the screen. The point made by Peter Latham (1992, p. 257) applies just as much to work done in an information and communications technology (ICT) environment as elsewhere: 'it has become increasingly apparent that, faced with growing demands for assessment of attainment, the teacher who values and encourages children's oral skills will always be more aware of what they really know, understand and are able to do.' With that in mind, the focus for the work with teachers and pupils described here was not on the technology, but on how it could be used to improve teaching and learning, in agreement with Collins *et al.* (1997, p. 100) who seek: 'to affirm the need for training and professional development, in particular for training programmes or events which focus on "how to do the job better" (Clegg 1994) rather than the technology and how to operate it.'

This chapter describes the use of a newly developed program, *Fabula*, in a primary school in Swansea. The aim is to focus on the 'ordinary' use of such software and to highlight the integral role played by talk in its success.

The Fabula Project

The *Fabula Project* ran for two years from 1998–2000 and was funded by the European Commission. It was a multi-disciplinary project, involving researchers in the fields of language education, typography and graphical communication, and human–computer interface design and software developers. Its aim was to develop an easy-to-use program to enable primary school teachers and pupils to make and read bilingual multimedia story-books. A further aim was to support, enhance and promote the use of the lesser-used languages of Europe, with partners working in and with schools teaching Basque, Catalan, Frisian, Irish, Welsh, Dutch, English, French, and Spanish. (For further details of the project visit the Fabula website: http://www.fabula.eu.org from where the software can be downloaded free of charge.)

In the UK, the researchers from Reading and Brighton Universities worked with three primary schools (two English-medium and one Welsh-medium) in Swansea, and this chapter reports on the work carried out with a Year 5 class in one of the English-medium schools.

The school

St Illtyd's is a well-resourced primary school in terms of information and communications technology (ICT), with a head teacher who has a clear vision of the importance of its role in children's education and teachers who are keen to integrate it into their work with pupils. The children are generally regular and confident ICT users and many of them have computers at home. The teachers we met would all describe themselves as 'inexperienced users' though their actual facility belied this: their commitment to ongoing professional development and eagerness to include ICT in their work with pupils would also suggest that they were relatively advanced. That said, not all of them were familiar with all the technology they would need to draw on to make full use of the Fabula software, such as digital photography, scanning software and digital sound recording. These teachers, however, were able to draw on expertise within their school or from the St Helen's Welsh Centre to enable them to carry out such tasks. None of the teachers were initially confident about their ability to use the Fabula software, but their experience of using computers as an everyday part of their work meant that they were cautious rather than anxious and, once they had a clear grasp of how to use it, they generated ideas about how it could fit in with their curriculum plans. Their commitment was central to our ability to work through difficulties caused by the relative instability of the software, which was still very much in development during the period described. For this we owe them and their pupils an enormous debt of thanks.

The *Branwen* story

The class had been working on a school drama project developing their own play based on the ancient Welsh myth of Branwen. A group of children from the school had been involved in performing the play in the Millennium Dome in London, an experience that had generated a great deal of activity and excitement. The pupils had all written their own version of the story and they were now going to produce a bilingual multimedia version using the *Fabula* software.

Their teacher, Alison Howells, carefully structured the activity with the children. First, she read them one of the versions written by a pupil (David) and discussed the significant ways in which a continuous prose account might vary from a multimedia version.

When she asked the children what would happen if she simply flowed the story into the software template one child replied, 'It wouldn't be fair, miss.' The implication seemed to be that they – the children, not the teacher – should be involved in the use of the software. This appeared to be confirmed when she asked, 'What's wrong with it now?' (meaning in its current format) and was greeted with the response, 'We haven't all agreed on it.' They were focusing on issues of authorship of the text whereas Alison's agenda was more about the layout of the piece. She asked them to, 'tell me the difference between stories we write in our books and the story we're going to write in the program'. This produced such reasonable responses as:

P1:   It's on paper.
P2:   The way it's written; it's in a different order of what happened.
P3:   We need to make it more exciting.

Alison was essentially seeking to elicit responses about the differences in the two media, but the children seemed more focused on the content. She again held up David's version and asked them to compare this with their recollection of a Fabula story they had read previously:

A.H.:   Did you see reams and reams of writing?
P1:   No.
P2:   Pictures.
P3:   Paragraphs.

The structural difference she was evidently looking for was the 'page per event' division which is a clear feature of the multimedia tool.

The children were then asked to recall events from the legend and to decide which ones they would include in their multimedia version. The teacher skilfully reactivated the children's knowledge of the story and used their responses as part of an initial editing process as they made decisions about which events were essential to the story and which could be safely left out. Naturally, this process involved a great deal of open-ended talk as the teacher elicited contributions from the children, sought their comments and evaluations as to the significance of the events, recording them on the board so that they were available for future reference.

Once they had collectively agreed on the key scenes and characters she assigned one scene each to groups of five or six pupils and one group was given the task of creating an introductory page on each character in the story – a multimedia version of the *dramatis personae*.

They further discussed the features that they would need to bear in mind in a multimedia environment, such as the layout of the page, what sounds might need to be incorporated and how they might produce them. The discussion and improvisation of sound effects (battle raging; cauldrons cracking; waves breaking; gossips whispering, etc.) provided not only a humorous interlude to the proceedings but also drew further attention to the multimedia dimensions of their literacy and the expanded range of resources that the term now implies. As Kress (1998, p. 58) points out:

The landscape of communication of the 1990s is very different; it is irrefutably a multisemiotic one; and the visual mode in particular has already taken on a central position in this landscape. Other modes are also becoming more significant as forms of representation and of communication than they have been in the more recent past. Sound … whether in the form of 'soundtrack', 'music', or 'background noise', is one of these …

Having identified the key scenes and the verbal, visual and audio resources they would require, Alison acted as the recorder of their collected efforts, organising their contributions under specific headings on the board so that they could refer back to them in the course of their work.

The pupils were first set to work on producing an English version of their text. It was stressed that they had to bear in mind that they would also be responsible for producing the Welsh translation and they should construct their English text accordingly. This 'restriction' on their writing led to some very interesting work in terms of language development. As one might expect, the students largely ignored their teacher's injunction and simply got down to writing the most exciting version they could. Discussions of their initial efforts and the problems of translation into Welsh, made it clear that some of the pupils perceived the challenges of translation in terms of vocabulary only:

P1:   She wore elegant clothes.
P2:   Do they have 'elegant' in Welsh?

They did not readily recognise that the real problems they would face would be with translating new and complex structures. Talking explicitly to them about these problems, however, at the same time as pointing out the availability of bilingual dictionaries to solve difficulties at the word level, made the real challenges more clear to them.

A further issue arose in terms of the length of the text they wrote, which also threatened to exceed their Welsh resources.

The drafting process proved to be a very valuable part of the exercise. We witnessed the first session and then the third in a sequence of lessons. The English text we saw on the latter visit had become much more concise, as can be seen from these two extracts:

First draft
Bran went to the battlefield with 500 men. You would be able only to hear 'For Wales!' and screaming. Mofuloch waited with 500 men also. Wales were behind because Ireland had the cauldron of rebirth so Nisien tried to smash it, but he died. The battle was tiring, long. Blood stained the grass and bodies scattered the battlefield.

Second draft
The battle had begun. Ireland had the advantage because of the cauldron. The battle was long, tiring, and bloody.

This process was extremely useful not only in terms of first language development but also in terms of the value of translation/parallel authoring in the second language, as the children had to consider and deploy their linguistic resources with immense care. The talk surrounding their competence in Welsh and how that impacted on the development of their English text was crucial in producing a balanced bilingual text. The integration of these language skills with the demands of the software and the restricted screen space for each language led the pupils to refine the text into more manageable chunks.

In the course of two further visits we observed the group of children who were working on the cast of characters. They were engaged in entering their English and Welsh versions into the two text panels and importing images which they had previously scanned from a book. (Other groups were going to use digital photographs taken from a school performance of the story.)

Again, a limitation of the software (the fixed size of the image screen) was turned to advantage as the children had to crop the image to fit the screen. They did this with an impressive mixture of technical and aesthetic aplomb. For example, they had to crop an image of a woman's face to fit a format that was much longer than it was wide. After some discussion (supported by one of the researchers, John Knight), they decided to go for a close-up of the character's rather mournful eyes which beautifully complemented the way they had described her in the accompanying text:

P1:   It's got to be wide across.
P2:   We could only scan a little bit.
JK: Just choose part of the picture.
(they select a narrow strip of the image, focusing on the eyes)
P1:   Whoa, that's good.
P3:   Perfect.
P2:   Shall we ask Miss if it's good?

Miss certainly agreed that it was good, as did we.

It was interesting to note the cinematic quality of their choice. It reflected the increasing role the visual aspect is playing in the construction of texts and the importance of incorporating such changes into an expanded view of the literacy curriculum. This is argued for by Kress and van Leeuwen (1996) and Kress (1997, p. 160) when he writes:

> Electronic media – as well as new technologies of printing make images into a much more available, accessible and *usable* mode of communication than they have been – in 'the West' at any rate for several hundred years. That is having far-reaching effects on language, especially in its written form, which have only just begun and are likely to alter the place and valuation of writing in far-reaching ways.

It is also worth noting that, while flicking through the book searching for an appropriate image, one of the girls was reminded of a sad song sung by the character in their version of the play and she began to sing it very quietly as they turned the pages. Her friends gradually joined in. It seemed clear that the space the teacher had created for children to work around the computer away from the rest of the class was one in which their personal responses were also allowed free rein – not necessarily something one readily associates with ICT activities – a salient reminder of Roy Corden's (1992, p. 184) view of the role of the teacher in encouraging pupil–pupil talk:

> Being an expert is about more than possessing and transmitting information. It's about understanding how children learn, encouraging and creating effective learning climates, developing interpersonal relationships and knowing when and how to intervene productively.

This view is supported in the ICT context by Collins *et al.* (1997, p. 122):

> The engagement with multimedia material for which we are arguing is one where learners interact with each other as much as the material … we are not so much interested in the number of clicks learners make when they explore material but the quality of their thinking and talking.

The *Fabula Project* required children (and teachers) to employ their ICT skills to the full. The learning outcomes involved both ICT and literacy but success of the project was dependent on purposeful talk. At each stage in the development of the multimedia story, talk played an essential role as demonstrated when pupils:

- discussed with their teacher how the project should proceed;
- retold the events in the original story in order to decide which parts to include in the multimedia version;

- negotiated with each other and agreed on the story;
- responded to, commented upon and evaluated the work in progress;
- discussed the layout of the page, sound effects and how they might produce them;
- listened and responded to their teacher and the Fabula adviser;
- talked about their competence in Welsh and how that influenced the production of a balanced bilingual text.

It was particularly encouraging observing the way in which the technical and textual dimensions were not treated separately but as part of a whole, and a synaesthetic whole at that. Teachers and pupils alike were quite naturally drawing upon the demands and opportunities of the verbal, visual, and aural alike in their conversations about how a multimedia text might be made.

Lewis Carroll has Alice ponder at one point, 'What is the use of a book without pictures or conversations?' The answer that the question is becoming increasingly redundant is one that is emerging from our primary schools. IT's not all talk, nor should all the talk be about IT, but it is certainly worth talking about.

References

Birkerts, S. (1994) *The Gutenberg Elegies – The State of reading in an electronic age.* London: Faber and Faber.

Clegg, C. (1994) 'Psychology and information technology: the study of cognition in organisations', *British Journal of Psychology* **85**, 449–77.

Collins, J., Hammond, M. and Wellington, J. (1997) *Teaching and Learning with Multimedia.* London: Routledge.

Cordon, R. (1992) 'The role of the teacher', in Norman, K. (ed.) *Thinking Voices: the work of the National Oracy Project,* 172–85. Sevenoaks: Hodder & Stoughton.

Edwards, T. (1992) 'Teacher talk and pupil competence', in Norman, K. (ed.) *Thinking Voices: the work of the National Oracy Project,* 235–41. Sevenoaks: Hodder & Stoughton.

Kress, G. (1997) *Before Writing – rethinking the paths to literacy.* London: Routledge.

Kress, G. (1998) 'Visual and verbal modes of representation in electronically mediated communication: the potentials of new forms of text', in Snyder, I. (ed.) *Page to Screen: taking literacy into the electronic era,* 53–79. London: Routledge.

Kress, G. and van Leeuwen, T. (1996) *Reading Images – The Grammar of Visual Design.* London: Routledge.

Latham, P. (1992) 'Oracy and the National Curriculum', in Norman, K. (ed.) *Thinking Voices: the work of the National Oracy Project,* 256–62. Sevenoaks: Hodder & Stoughton.

Lachs, V. (2000) *Making Multimedia in the Classroom: a teacher's guide.* London: Routledge/Falmer.

Visit the Fabula website at: www.fabula.eu.org

Part 3

Imagination and creativity

Chapter 11

Foundations for talk – Speaking and listening in the early years classroom

Lesley Clark

Children talking confidently with each other and with informed and sensitive adults about what they experience, feel and think, drives learning in early years classrooms. The centrality of talk is all pervading. Issues about the quality of interactions and opportunities for talk are of fundamental concern to teachers in planning a motivating learning environment. Where this is not the case reflects, perhaps, current concerns with recorded and measurable evidence of teaching the skills for reading and writing. An implicit belief that effective talk is crucial for effective learning must be an explicit part of the planning of every time-pressured teaching day. It is especially important to devote attention to discovering and nurturing each child's 'personal voice' – a treasure trove of understandings and emotions which give vital insights into the child's understanding and knowledge of literacies within and beyond the classroom.

Transitions from home to school lay the foundations for how each individual will respond to new challenges in learning. Unless children feel confident that their personal voice will be listened to, respected and made relevant, there is a danger that active learning will diminish. Through exploring, playing and refining, children follow their own logic in learning. Teacher modelling and supporting, listening and understanding, provides patterns on which new learning can be built. Talk is also the vehicle for establishing caring and enthusiastic learning and social relationships within the classroom. This chapter explores ways in which we can listen to, learn from and teach effective talk. Through personal and collected observations and research, I will offer examples of how talk sustains all learning – giving particular emphasis to early writing development.

Routine talk

Talk is the medium for establishing shared routines which themselves provide space for nurturing talk. Simply recognising how precious these routines are is the first step into

maximising their potential. The start of every day sets the pattern for classroom relationships. A staggered arrival of children to the classroom allows opportunities for
personal talk and observations. This may be a time when children are still anxious about
coming to school. They will need their feelings acknowledged and addressed promptly
and sensitively. The teacher might help articulate and explore negative feelings, while
using the security of daily routines and responsibilities to ease the child into the school
day. Peer support is invaluable here, being effective because teachers have modelled
and discussed this caring role. There are many specifically 'literate' activities amongst
morning routines, such as:

> discussing family and home events;
> using name cards for a variety of activities;
> setting and responding to simple alphabetic or word puzzles;
> different forms of greetings;
> selecting and discussing material for home reading;
> sharing retellings of favourite rhymes, songs and stories;
> celebrating home community literacies;
> creating texts in the design and writing area;
> providing routine information and answering the register;
> sharing messages, notes and lists.

All such activities offer opportunities for incidental observation and learning. In the
informal conversations which punctuate these routines, there is a genuine purpose and
interest in questions asked and details given. This serves to enrich language and to
affirm trusting and positive relationships. However, early mornings are a peak time for
teacher attention, with administrative messages and parental concerns competing against
calm interaction with children. Sharing responsibilities with colleagues, targeting focus
children and having a clear but sympathetic whole-school policy regarding parental
access to teachers can alleviate these pressures. Quality personal talk a couple of days
a week may need to be balanced by more independent activities at other times. Planned
observation also allows teachers to reflect upon children's preferred learning styles and
social patterns. After all, we all know adults who have very definite morning behaviour!
Our welcoming, chattering morning routines should ease children into acceptable
patterns of interaction while offering genuine choice to cater for their diverse responses
and interests in the shared learning environment.

Effective classroom management and organisation help to teach and nurture effective
oral skills. Routines such as settling on the carpet, answering the register and moving
around, initiating and clearing away activities, sharing ideas, stories and songs can all be
varied and energised by child-interest, humour and quirky phrases. These regular procedures have implications beyond their functional objectives. They are very visible parts
of shared understandings created through speech and demonstration. Where possible,
children should have a real say in and responsibility for these times, enabling them to
demonstrate and consolidate their skills and sense of belonging. Time spent in a nursery soon highlights the ability of even very young children to participate actively in and
to take responsibility for learning routines in a variety of ways.

Playing with words

Shared phrases, jokes, puns and rhymes celebrate class communities and encourage an
atmosphere ringing with the rhythm and music of words! The fun and energy generated

by such playfulness mask the serious benefits in terms of linguistic understanding, phonic and spelling knowledge. Experimentation will be demonstrated through playful routines:

answering the register in different ways;
finding rhymes and rhythms in clapping names, TV personalities, sweets, etc.;
issuing routine instructions and requests to line up, clear up, etc., in rhyme;
having a daily slot for reciting songs and rhymes;
learning and inventing playground raps and skipping games;
providing daily written word searches and puzzles for each other;
providing detective games for alphabet and dictionary materials;
weekly word wizards, sharing the discovery of patterns and phrases from texts;
word wall writers who provide a decorative display with analogies and rimes;
techno talk – words specific to crazes and hobbies.

Looking and listening for patterns, for experiments with language and jokes, can sharpen attention and motivate the risk-taking necessary for literacy learning. Children love alliterative jingles and rhymes involving their names, labelling routine objects and actions.

'If you're wearing blue, you know what to do,
If you're wearing grey, don't take all day!'
Amazing Amanda! Brilliant Bruno! Crazy Christopher ...
'Quickly, quietly standing tall, we're all marching to the hall.'

Teachers will make their own judgements about how much 'media talk' and childish humour to encourage in different contexts. Perhaps tapping into some of the silliness and rowdiness of the playground may provide new openings for literacy learning. Recent research has suggested that, where teachers observe and develop what seems like 'aggressive' play, children swiftly move into acceptable and sophisticated scripts (Holland 1999).

Developing a personal voice

If teachers are to motivate children and to help them develop positive attitudes to learning, then they must listen to and nurture each child's 'personal voice'. A child's sense of identity, of belonging within classroom relationships and of being valued is linked to confidence in their 'personal' voice. It is a challenge for the teacher to tap into and support spontaneous individual talk, whilst also addressing learning needs through more structured interaction. Although teachers may plan the use of key words and phrases to support concepts covered and key questions to assess understanding, they are aware that deeper learning requires sensitive response during genuine interaction. Children need to use talk for a range of purposes and to gain an appreciation of the needs of their audiences. They need a range of learning experiences to achieve this including; contrasting stimulus for talk, quiet talk, private talk, focused group talk, spontaneous collaboration and more structured whole-class interaction, as well as varying social contexts for talk.

High/Scope principles

Talk is a powerful way of fostering positive attitudes, motivating and engaging children in their learning environment. Sessions following High/Scope principles (Brown 1990), in which children have to make and reflect upon real decisions in their learning, illustrate the potential sophistication of young learners. The detail and accuracy of their planning increases over time, as does the quality and sensitivity of reflection. At reviewing circles, children learn to respect individual differences, to listen intently as one peer describes how a bridge was successfully constructed, another why original plans regarding small-world play proved too ambitious and a third recites a collaboratively constructed rap! The teacher oversees and models, gives space and opportunity, focuses praise and constructive support. She also demonstrates active listening skills and has legitimate opportunities to ask real questions.

Personal, social and health education (PSHE) programmes, building upon the *Curriculum guidance for the Foundation Stage* (QCA and DfEE 2000) and the QCA guidelines *Teaching Speaking and Listening at Key Stages 1 and 2* (QCA 1999), help with the planning of teaching talk.

Structured techniques, such as Circle Time and paired work, are needed to develop effective oral collaboration. Such activities take time to establish through modelling and frequent revision. Pairs could complete a short task, sequence pictures, make decisions, present information, listen to and summarise each other's news – having seen such skills modelled and discussed by the teacher. Whole-class sessions will also provide security in familiar communication patterns – listening to each other and learning the language of effective questioning. Young children love to follow patterns of praise, as a four-year-old demonstrated in responding to her peer: 'That's a good question, Jessie! No, I didn't see dolphins on the beach.' They also learn to limit the scope of their contributions to match the context: 'When I had … when my sister's friends … I went on the beach to my Nanny's house.' However, some personalities may find the 'routine' intimacy of whole-class circles inappropriate for developing their personal voices, so less daunting alternatives need to be created. It is often through play that these skills will be practised and consolidated.

Talk and literacy learning

The National Literacy Strategy (NLS) prioritises talk, placing a heavy emphasis on whole-class interaction. It encourages the use of a range of techniques including, listening, pausing, echoing and clarifying children's responses. The benefits of modelling and discussing reading and writing are also made very clear. However, sufficient flexibility and delegation of control to provide for genuine talk should accompany discussions about reading and writing. This ideal becomes harder to achieve with increasing levels of formality, pressure on time and size of group. Children will learn that there are different acceptable styles of conversation in different contexts; the challenge is for the teacher to demonstrate consistent respect and support for individuals throughout. Giving children the responsibility to make choices in their reading and writing requires sensitive listening and response to what they say. Teachers must plan regular time for children to talk about their interests and concerns, and to discuss their approaches and attitudes to reading and writing. Silent reading routines, book buddies, and opportunities to discuss text selections and respones with others are, ideally, a feature of all early years classrooms. A similar approach needs to be adopted with writing so that spontaneous activities in the writing area, in role play, in journals and with friends, are validated through talk, modelling and positive feedback. The NLS also highlights the need to establish effective group interaction. This can be highly structured and focused or more open-ended. Teachers who regularly provide informal contexts can gain from joining in during group interaction, listening to children as they talk and work, before deciding how to lead them forward. Children need the experience of taking different roles within a group, as do teachers! Pressures make it tempting to lead, direct and question without giving children the space to demonstrate their understanding. As teachers listen to what children are saying they gain useful insights into literacy learning.

The language of play and role play

Curriculum guidance for the Foundation Stage. (QCA and DfEE 2000) makes play a priority as a medium for learning, yet it can be easily marginalised in the busy early years classroom. Research into children's play repeatedly demonstrates the richness and range of language employed: 'by engaging in children's story making in an active and participatory manner I have uncovered depths of understanding and complexity of ideas that are difficult to tap in the ordinary everyday activities of the best classroom' (Hendy 1995). Young children may use a stylised running commentary to sustain their individual play. This includes singing, rhyming and gesture together with descriptive detail of what and how they are directing the action in their storying. Thus, a child playing with 'Brio-Mec' hums and sings the journey his train takes, using repetition and noises to punctuate the script. Collaborative play and role play offers authentic purposes for exploring different types of talk. Negotiating and confirming roles and responsibilities, sharing resources and deciding how they are going to be played with, are very demanding. Such play is often fluid and requires frequent re-directing, so arguing and persuading, reaffirming and explaining are required to sustain it. Negotiating and affirming story lines allows children to direct their play. By sharing in and celebrating these play-narratives, teachers can make links with the patterned language and structures of shared readings and storytellings. Observing retellings, often supported by puppets or props, provides teachers with insights into children's understanding and enjoyment of story. Take, for example, this extract from a video *The Foundations of Learning* (Barrs *et al.* 1999), which shows a group of nursery children collaboratively reconstructing the story of Three Billy Goats Gruff using a wooden brick bridge and a mask for the Troll:

Child A: Who's that tripping-trap over my bridge?
Child B: It's only me – little one.
Child C: AAAAHHH! Leave my BROTHER alone!
(The voice of Little Billy Goat surprises all! The troll prompts goat on bridge.)
Child A: You've got to say 'Wait for that one' Go on …
Child B: No you …
Child C: LEAVE MY BROTHER ALONE!
             (This impassioned plea leads a passing boy to intervene.)
Child D: I'm gonna see what's going on … (He kicks wooden block bridge that is supporting troll) I knocked your house down.

Acting out stories provides safe ways to explore strong emotions, supported by an attentive adult whose empathy (and sense of humour) allows her or him to maximise the experiences for the children.

Role play provides children with opportunities to demonstrate their understanding by tapping into experiences, voices and contexts beyond the classroom. Messages, lists, receipts, cards, invitations, official forms, environmental print or finding out what's on television invite the exploration of 'everyday' literacy. This realism energises role play with a range of purposes and audiences. By involving children in initiating and resourc-ing role play areas, teachers can rehearse scenarios and highlight and model literacy acts. Repetition and patterning of play facilitate teacher intervention, often in role, to extend the learning, while ensuring control remains with the children. These factors combine to motivate children towards taking risks and exploring literacy in ways they may find problematic in more structured work. Hall and Robinson (1995) provide exam-ples of the skilled use of role play to support writing, such as the teacher writing in role. Whole-class talk can then be used to validate and extend the play.

Writing and talking

Teachers provide steps into the writing process for children by talking about writing and demonstrating it in different contexts. Classroom dialogue and secure relationships help the teacher to establish what each child knows about writing, and their motivation and attitude to writing. The work of researchers such as Pahl (1999), Kress (1997) and Nutbrown (1997), alerts teachers to the dangers of a narrow interpretation of what liter-acy is. It is not easy for young children to articulate their thoughts about writing. Yet unreflective use of metalanguage could mask misconceptions. Asked about the purposes of writing, a group of five-year-olds demonstrated a confused set of ideas, narrowed by a focus on words rather than the purposes of composing texts:

Jamila:	It's so you know things, so you read.
Carl:	I do writing at home, like saying and just writing words like 'the' and 'Roger' ... 'Cos it makes help you learn stuff.
Charlie:	I do some joined-up writing ... I do loops.
Carl:	'Cos if you didn't know how to write, you wouldn't know the words.
Jamila:	I don't like writing much 'cos it's very hard work. You have to do lots of remembering.
Charlie:	I done my writing by I just thinked my brain.
Child:	You have to write about your weekend and if you can't remember that is really hard.
Adult:	What do you do then?
Child:	I ... went... to... i... ll... fr... a... combe... I... ll... fr...
Adult:	What are you doing?
Child:	Stretching the word.
Adult:	Why?
Child:	So you can hear the words.

Effective teachers must devote much energy into establishing positive attitudes through giving status to the varied ways children engage in the writing process. Ideally, children who feel like writers, write regularly because they are genuinely motivated and are confident to do so, having been taught supportive strategies. The combination of emer-gent and 'correct' models and scripts presents a delicate and an ambitious balance. The demands of writing seem too great if young children regularly fear negative feedback from tasks to which they feel no personal commitment. Observing and talking to chil-dren as they write in different situations – independently, collaboratively, in role, both directed and spontaneously – allows teachers to develop a picture of individual writers. Motivation must also be linked to clarity of the writing purpose and the teacher's honesty in confining responses to this agreed focus.

Observing young writers

Contriving audiences and drawing children to structured writing tasks provides many challenges in the nursery. For example, one teacher shared her obvious love of Eric Carle books imaginatively with her class and the children's responses mirrored her enthusiasm. However, a device to encourage a written response to Mr Busy, a visiting spider who had sent the children in spidery scrawl urging them to help him 'write better', failed to inspire. This was especially true of boys called away from their play-worlds and construction. 'It's my turn when I come back!' summed up the real focus of their interest. Unsurprisingly, their stay at the 'writing table' was brief, 'Done it!' being one child's hasty response. Another, Sean, sat listlessly repeating 'I can't do writing!' until the teacher interjected with 'Have a go, write your name'. Sean was more interested in having a conversation with an adult observer about playing N64 games with his Dad before he mentioned spiders. Then he said, 'When I saw a spider when I was a baby, I didn't run away'. After bouncing Mr Busy (strategically suspended above the table), he suggested that the 'spider message' should be to 'send a message to my Mum and be careful don't fall over someone's foot'. He eventually elected to trace over the web design which had been faintly copied onto the letter paper, and to write one symbol in each section of the web, saying eventually 'I'm doing one more letter'. The Mr Busy stimulus for writing needed more teacher talk and flexibility. Talking through Mr Busy's lack of confidence, could both establish empathy and appeal to the children's writing expertise. Yet finding the right moment to lead children to attempt a writing 'task' is not easy. Perhaps asking children to write how Mr. Busy could build a Lego web or use the water-tray would have been more successful. Listening for leads, such as that offered by Sean's bravado as a baby, is also crucial. Adult encouragement, modelling and feedback during the writing process are a vital ingredient in motivating young authors.

Having gained the confidence to write independently, most children relish opportunities to share and discuss their work with chosen peers and adults. A personal response from a trusted audience is also a key feature of 'interactive writing' between adult and child (Hall 2000). These may look like conversational 'letters', but the skill is to promote equality and honesty so that the child writer takes the initiative, asking the adult questions and directing writing towards subjects of personal interest. Hall amusingly and sympathetically exemplifies the tenacity and confidence of children liberated by interactive writing. The teacher's sensitive response provides models and supports and affirms the genuineness of the learning relationship, while leaving decisions and directions for the child writer.

Talk is an important tool for crafting ideas for writing, and for following shared supports in *how* to write. Oral rehearsal, patterned talk and repetition help sustain a message in the memory as the child writes. This behaviour also helps to shut out classroom distractions as children focus on known words, and link sounds to symbols. Guided writing allows teachers to interact during the writing process and also to punctuate it with group discussions and feedback to affirm each writer's message. For every sentence on the page, there will be dozens of hidden utterances, thoughts and details – for example, from Hannah, aged five, 'I did get up I went to the shops and got some more clothes with my Mum and my Tom'. Hannah spoke animatedly about her shopping trip and her conversation included accurate details of environmental print, shop brandings, etc. Talk helps ease the tensions and potential frustration caused by transcriptional demands upon young writers. Children should be offered different situations, including play and less structured tasks, in which to discuss their writing with each other. It is important to use drawing and other media to convey messages. An overemphasis on writing will reduce opportunities to open up dialogue about a child's ideas buried in pictures or models.

Home–school relations

Schools need to listen and respond to, as well as inform, the communities they serve. This is particularly crucial in the early years (Weinberger 1996, Dombey and Meek Spencer 1994, Hall 1987, Nutbrown and Hannon 1997). Home visits can provide rich insights for teachers and parents and offer non-threatening opportunities to explain school approaches to learning. For example, what counts as early writing development can be discussed in an attempt to erase unhelpful myths and for the teachers to appreciate the impact of different cultural literacy norms. Opportunities to further home–school links can be extended through lively workshops, special events and parent-teacher meetings. Useful resources for home, such as *Storysacks* (Griffiths 1997) – especially those created with local community involvement – provide models and props to stimulate a range of language activities which underpin reading and writing. Asking questions and playing games, explaining the logic of rules and the intricacies of plot, provide a platform for learning and opportunities for shared writing at home. Retelling and revisiting favourite texts in a variety of ways, both at home and at school, provides essential experiences with written language and story structure. These practices help to sustain constructive dialogue about literacy between school and home. Children will be encouraged to share activities and show writing produced at home, especially when work is celebrated and displayed in class. The special bond of enjoying reading and writing in the intimacy of home can be celebrated in class. Community languages and events should also be powerfully reinforced by finding opportunities for parents and carers to come in and share their expertise in the classroom. The different spheres of home and school can become united through talk.

Teachers talking

In addition to the provision of talk experiences for children, teachers must think about how they speak to children. Teachers must be aware that choice of words, clarity of structure, body language and tactics for engaging and responding to children will influence children. Like other aspects of teaching, the ideal of offering a balanced range of approaches with the flexibility to adapt to children's responses, requires ongoing attention. Planned time for observing and listening to children is an essential aspect of teaching, requiring sensitive monitoring and reflection. Knowledge gained about learning styles, preferences and understanding of literacy practices then needs to be translated into planned teaching opportunities and outcomes. This requires rigour, energy and teamwork. Ideally, other adults working in collaboration to build up a more comprehensive picture of the child learner support early years teachers. A variety of adult personalities and perspectives, sharing a clear vision of why and how they develop talk with children, provides a rich basis for teaching.

A great deal can be gained from the regular sharing of experiences and ideas between teachers. Talking through a typical day with colleagues might suggest ways to improve provision. There may be an overemphasis on one approach, for example, when most interactions focus on quick mental recall in question and answer sessions. A supportive comment from a colleague can help rectify any imbalance in planning. By observing colleagues and feeding back ideas, teachers can develop strategies to maximise effective interaction. Teachers may use a variety of multi-sensory teaching methods; contexts and types of communication patterns also need to be varied.

Conclusion

Vibrant classroom talk presents challenges and pleasure for busy teachers. The facts that talk is difficult to quantify, plan for and measure, can lead to its becoming overshadowed by other aspects of learning. Lip-service is paid to the centrality of talk without adequate support for teachers to develop classroom practice. There is an urgent need for considered reflection on how to listen for, establish and nurture effective dialogue for learning. Personal and social talk are vital elements in achieving this goal but all types of talk must be harnessed to support an active learning environment. At a time when teachers face many pressures to conform to particular methods for teaching literacy, the deeper issues involved in managing interactive, discursive classrooms, must be acknowledged. If there is too early a focus on didactic teaching and measurable outcomes for reading and writing, the sensitivity and respect needed to acknowledge and develop individual voices could be threatened. Teachers must feel confident about exercising their professional judgement in response to the needs, voiced and unvoiced, of young learners in their care. Judgements should be made within contexts that afford talk the time and flexibility it deserves.

References

Brown, M. (1990) *An Introduction to High/Scope approach in the National Curriculum.* Michigan: HighScope Press.

DfEE (1999) *National Literacy Strategy leaflets 1, 2 and 3. Training Module: Teaching and Learning Strategies.* London: HMSO.

Dombey, H. and Meek Spencer, M. (eds) (1994) *First Steps Together: Home–School Early Literacy in European Contexts.* Stoke-on-Trent: Trentham Books.

Griffiths, N. (1997) *Storysacks: A starter information pack.* Swindon: Storysack Enterprises.

Hall, N. (1987) *The Emergence of Literacy: Young children's developing understanding of reading and writing.* London: David Fulton Publishers.

Hall, N. (2000) *Interactive writing in the primary school.* Reading: Reading and Language Information Centre.

Hall, N. and Robinson, A. (1995) *Exploring Writing and Play in the Early Years.* London: David Fulton Publishers.

Hendry, L. (1995) *Playing, Role Play and Dramatic Activity in the Early Years,* Vol. 15 No. 2. Stoke-on-Trent: Trentham Books.

Holland, P. (1999) 'Just pretending: developing boy's dramatic play in the nursery', *Language Matters,* Spring, 2–5.

Kress, G. (1997) *Before Writing: rethinking the paths to literacy.* London: Routledge.

Nutbrown, C. (1997) *Recognising Early Literacy Development: Assessing children's achievements.* London: Paul Chapman.

Nutbrown, C. and Hannon, P. (eds) (1997) *Preparing for Early Literacy Education with Parents.* Nottingham: REAL Project/NES Arnold.

Pahl, K. (1999) *Transformations: Meaning making in nursery education.* Stoke-on-Trent: Trentham Books.

QCA (1999) *Teaching Speaking and Listening in Key Stages 1 and 2.* London: QCA.

QCA and DfEE (2000) *Curriculum guidance for the Foundation Stage.* London: QCA and DfEE.

Weinberger, J. (1996) *Literacy goes to School.* London: Paul Chapman.

Video

Barrs, M. *et al.* (1999) *The Foundations of Learning.* London: Centre for Language in Primary Education (CLPE).

Chapter 12

'Is that the little pig?' – Using toy telephones in the early years classroom

Julia Gillen, with Liz Stone and Liz Cosier

It is Circle Time at the beginning of the afternoon in Mrs Stone's Reception classroom. Mrs Stone sits beside a table with two telephones on it and shows a large book already familiar to the children, *The Three Little Pigs*. She asks, 'Who's going to ring us up today?'

The children call out, 'The big bad wolf!'

'Let's see if the big bad wolf can persuade a pig to let him in. Who's going to be a little pig?' All hands wave. Hannah is selected and moves forward to sit in one of the chairs.

> Mrs Stone picks up one of the telephones, 'Brrrrr…ing!'
> Hannah picks up her phone, 'Hello?'
> A growly voice says, 'Is that the little pig?'
> 'Yes, that's me.'
> 'This is the big wolf. I just wondered if you, little pig, little pig, would let me come in?'
> 'No, no, not by the hair of my chinny chin chin!'

'Mr Wolf' makes an aside to the children: 'I wonder if I could huff and puff?'
'Yes! Try!'

> Into the phone, 'Little pig, could I come round and clean your chimney?'
> Hannah responds bravely: 'No Mr Wolf, I don't trust you!'
> 'Oh little pig, I don't have any friends.'
> 'I don't care!'
> 'Couldn't I just come round and give you a hand with your work? Which house do you live in?'
> 'The brick house, but I won't let you in.'

The children listen enthralled to the unfolding dialogue and several take turns in participating, including those children who are sometimes shy in speaking especially in front of one another. Yet this enjoyable scenario draws them in. Later that afternoon, while the children take part in a variety of activities, most of them choose to spend some time at that table, reworking the dialogues, inventing new twists to the story and sometimes referring to the book.

Semi-structured play activities in Mrs Stone's classroom include the use of play telephones in a number of situations, in either a central or relatively peripheral role. Mrs

Stone, convinced of the benefits of harnessing imaginative play towards the development of children's orality and literacy, often begins by modelling a role, ensuring
through discussion and observation that the children involved have the necessary understanding to then enact and develop the role play themselves. For example, simple play
with park animals on a mat by a group of children was suddenly added to by one boy
importing an attacking dinosaur. Mrs Stone reacted as in a park keeper role, using a
phone to alert emergency services. The idea was later enthusiastically imitated and
refined by children long after Mrs Stone had moved to another part of the room.

A more developed and central role for the telephone over several weeks occurred in
the creation of an estate agency in the corner of the room. Discussions with the children led to an area furnished with a desk, computer, pair of portable toy phones and
portfolios and notices of actual estate agents' materials mixed with children's own
pictures. Although I watched children use the estate agency in only the second week of
its operation, I was impressed to see that a format of interaction had developed.
Typically four children played in the area at one time. In this example, Greg stood just
outside the agency and 'phoned in':

Greg:	Hello.
Beatrice:	Happy House estate agents.
Greg:	Hello. I'd like a house.
Beatrice:	What would you like in your house?

At the keyboard of the computer Tehmina sat ready to type. 'Three bedrooms,' began
Greg. 'Three bedrooms' sang Beatrice to Tehmina. A delay ensued while Tehmina
sought and copied the word 'bedrooms' which was one of those that had been put in
large lettering on a word card on the wall of the agency. When Tehmina had finished
Greg said to Beatrice, 'Four trees' and again the message was 'relayed'. This time
Tehmina did not have the word 'trees' in front of her to refer to but succeeded nevertheless. After Greg had finished giving his list of requirements he was told to come in
to the agency later. The list was printed out and placed in a folder.

At this stage the children began again by switching round roles. They had not yet, in
this the second week of estate agency play, learned to develop the estate agency function further. Mrs Stone was keen to take them to an estate agency if at all possible, or
at least to find other ways of encouraging further development. However, in the mean-
time this was an extremely encouraging beginning. The situation was interesting enough
to cause each of the children to have participated in the collaborative work necessary
to set up the agency and to go on to try out all the roles, each carefully typing the lists.
The telephone had a central function in focusing the talk onto the essential elements
that became written down and in establishing the participants' roles at the beginning of
each episode.

Why use telephones in the early years?

For several years I have been investigating the benefits of telephones in early years classrooms. I have visited many nurseries, classrooms and other out of home settings and
seen a great variety of ways in which they are used. I have also spent eight months in
a single nursery classroom trying out play opportunities, recording and analysing in
detail children's telephone talk. I am convinced that toy telephones are useful for the
reasons explained below.

Telephones appeal both to confident and less confident speakers

Confident children are often leaders of socio-dramatic play. They may well use the telephone and draw others into complex play that develops their oral skills. However, often toy telephones appeal to children who speak relatively little, especially sometimes in adults' presence. Tina, a twin who joined a nursery soon after her third birthday, tended to play alone and quietly. I had put a child-size phone box in the nursery. She began by lifting the phone and saying, 'Hello? Mum?' She listened intently and then muttered a few indistinct words into the telephone. After replacing the receiver she told another child waiting to use the phone: 'That my mum.'

Children's early telephone talk is patterned

Most children seem to begin telephone play by getting the beginnings and endings right. Many early pretence calls are similar to this one by Dennis, just after his third birthday:

'Hello'
'Hello'
'Bye'

A few days later this was one of his calls:

'Hello'
'Hello'
'Alright'
'OK Mum'
'Alright'
'Right Mum'
'Bye Mum'

Dennis's call might not seem overly impressive at first reading but in fact he is showing that he has a number of the skills involved in the accomplishment of a phone call (see Hopper 1992). Telephone talk, unlike face to face talk, needs firm openings and closings. On the phone, achieving mutual identification either explicitly or through voice recognition is a must – the use of 'Mum' of course is adequate. Taking turns is essential, and on the phone we cannot make use of non-verbal cues in doing this. The pauses in Dennis's speech here (as in all my transcriptions) are indicated by new lines; all his gaps are appropriate. Finally, it seems likely that his use of 'Right Mum' signals what Schegloff and Sacks (1973) called a 'pre-closing'. It has been observed from study of a large computerised corpus of spoken English that for many of us 'Right… ' is particularly often used to signal that we are coming to the end of a telephone call (Stenström 1987).

Telephone talk develops awareness and skill of register

An essential part of developing orality is of course the ability to select language appropriately according to context. My study of telephone talk in play shows that children are extending their register capabilities. Four-year-old Fiona began a pretend call to her mother as follows:

'Hello Mummy'
'Hello'
'Yes!' (with delight)
'I don't really'
(She continued with many isolated phrases generally apparently of a feedback nature, omitted here)

'Ta ra'
'Bye'
(Fiona blew kisses down the telephone before putting it down.)

On the other hand her demeanour and tone were quite different when pretending to phone the police:

'Oh double one oh double two oh double three' (muttered in a serious tone while dialling).
'Hello police!'
'Quickly there's a flash coming and it's going to hurt us!'
(Fiona then slammed the phone down quickly before rushing to a friend involved in the game in order to assure her that the police were on their way.)

Of course Fiona's call is not like a true emergency call. But she is showing signs of beginning to grasp features of the register of such calls – the summons of the correct agency and the demand for action (here truncated to 'quickly') followed immediately by a justification. The tone of such calls made by children is quite different from the casual chat of 'family' calls, and contains many attempts at appropriate technical terms. Edward made a long sequence of calls over several sessions in which he appeared to be trying to work out the problem of how the different emergency services link their work with one another. Here is one extract:

'Hello fireman.'
'Alright fireman. I'm the fireman bell on policeman to get the fire.'

Telephones appeal to boys and girls and are extremely flexible
I have found that telephones can appeal to girls and boys equally; for example the telephone box referred to above was equally commonly used by both sexes. Analysis of my data of telephone talk from young children has shown that the telephone talk of girls is not more complex or indeed simply more frequent than that of boys. I think that this could be linked with its great familiarity as a cultural object (even those children who do not have a phone at home know how to play with one) and its qualities as both a piece of technology and prompter for social conversation.

Mrs Stone's practice, where telephones are incorporated into a great variety of play situations, shows their enormous flexibility, although certainly how and where they are used may have an affect on their appeal to children of a particular gender. In another early years classroom, a telephone in 'The Three Bears' House' (Goldilocks was the theme) was used far more often by girls than boys.

Telephones may be useful in working with children with language difficulties
On this point I need to be extremely tentative, since, as far as I am aware, no research has been carried out which has specifically looked at the possibility of toy telephones being particularly beneficial for children with certain specific educational needs. Nevertheless I was not particularly surprised when early years teacher, Liz Cosier, reflecting upon her experiences with toy telephones remembered a child, Ryan, who particularly enjoyed the play area in his Reception/Year 1 classroom. He had special educational needs and, it seemed to Liz, his language was developing through spontaneous use during play more than in contexts where he seemed pressured to supply responses to a teacher's question. She had recorded one incident as follows:

Ryan loves using the phone. Today I heard him talking on the phone and asked him who he had called.
'The police.'
'Why?'
'The washing machine's broken.'
'Don't you want to phone the plumber then?'
'No, the police, the police are coming.'

Liz's impression that the telephone was particularly beneficial for Ryan is supported by two other cases. In the nursery classroom where I spent eight months, Darren received special staffing support in respect of language development and rarely uttered more than a monosyllable. However, his teachers were impressed by some of the recordings made in the telephone box I later showed them. At different, but appropriate times in play episodes with friends, Darren uttered openings, greetings, pre-closings and closings. Evans and Fuller (1996) in their study concerned with eliciting children's opinions of their nursery schools, found talking into telephones (across desks) a particularly useful way of encouraging conversation, and noted that the instrument seemed particularly to cause one child with special needs to display his orality to the full.

Other ways of using telephones

Phones in the 'reading corner'
In a large nursery classroom catering for over 50 children at the time, I saw that the toy telephones were not situated in the extensive 'home corner' as I might have expected, but rather in the 'reading corner'. The teacher explained that she saw the telephone as developing language and thus ideally situated with books.

Telephones and maths
Liz Cosier decided to make use of children's knowledge that one ordinarily 'dials' a number when using a telephone. While working on placement in a mixed Reception/Year 1 class she noticed that children in the home area enjoyed using disused real phones. She decided to encourage their use in an educational way, and made a poster, headed: 'Can you phone …' Underneath were names of popular characters such as Humpty Dumpty with a six-digit phone number beside each. Her subsequent observations demonstrated that the children now often carefully read the numbers and picked them out on the touch telephone.

Providing appropriate props
Such simple devices as placing notebooks and pencils near telephones are used by many teachers to encourage children in writing messages, lists and so on in their play. A key point here is that spending much money is not necessary; I think most children prefer discarded real telephones to expensive toys and enjoy attempting to use realistic props such as actual telephone directories.

Dressing-up clothes are extremely useful in stimulating role play that in turn impacts upon use of different registers. Shopkeeper talk or firefighter talk is more likely to be developed in increasingly complex ways if the children are offered some structuring of the experience by the teacher. This may include taking the children on an appropriate visit or using informative videos or texts with them, modelling roles and the provision of costumes with other props.

Conclusions

Mininni (1985) suggested that pretence telephoning is an extremely useful way of developing telephone discourse. Observations of his daughter led him to suggest that at the age of three when she found actual conversation on real phones difficult, she was nevertheless working on this 'specific dialogic sub-competence' as he characterises telephone discourse, in the pretence environment.

The telephone presents a challenge in comparison with face-to-face talk. Since the interlocutor is distanced and the environment is not shared then explicit reference needs to be made where gestures and non-verbal communication might otherwise suffice. My research leads me to believe that even in pretence children are practising this, and thus extending their language capabilities. An especially useful characteristic of telephone discourse is its patterning at beginnings and ends, surely often witnessed by most children from infancy, and thus giving them a template as it were with which to practice initially. Working with routines and formulaic phrases is a significant element in language acquisition, as of course has long been recognised in early years practice with the use of nursery rhymes, greeting routines, etc. (Lieven 1994, Gillen 1997).

Use of toy telephones can also have an affective quality and indeed has been used by professional play therapists (Spero 1993). I have often seen the non-threatening toy telephone harnessed by children in talk apparently partly aimed at self-reassurance, for example in the form of calm pretence calls to caregivers. This call was made by Peter, just after he had joined a new group:

'Hello Mum Mummy.'
'I'm doing fine at nursery I'm being good I'm going to play at pictures and put them in the post box but I'm in the house but I'm going to go in the house bye bye.'
'Bye bye.'

The case for recognising the capacity of pretence play, whether solitary or socio-dramatic, to contribute not just to children's emotional and social development but also to their orality and literacy, is one that has often been made (Moyles 1994, Hall and Robinson 1995). Yet I am concerned that under the pressure of recent curriculum developments and other pressures it is occasionally taking a back seat. Over the last year or so some of the teachers and assistants I have interviewed are now less engaged in focusing on play than they used to be, albeit making this change with reluctance. With the professionals who have contributed to this chapter, either directly or indirectly, I believe study of children's telephone talk to be revelatory of the power of play to enhance development in many respects including, centrally, language. The renowned educationalist Vygotsky wrote:

In play a child is always above his average age, above his daily behaviour; in play it is as though he were a head taller than himself. As in the focus of a magnifying glass, play contains all developmental tendencies in a condensed form; in play it is as though the child were trying to jump above the level of his normal behaviour. (Vygotsky 1967, p. 16)

With those words in mind, I end by relating a call made by Rowan, just after his fourth birthday.

Rowan, wearing an 'emergency' costume, enters the telephone box carrying a large telephone directory which he props up behind the phone.

'This page, oh, not that page, this page,' he says as he flicks through, as his friend Sam joins him in the box.

'We're going to get a new car,' Rowan tells Sam. (Sam replies but his response is not picked up by the microphone.)

Rowan dials, picking up the receiver as Sam talks. Rowan talks into the phone: 'Hello. Can we have a new car – me and Sam?'

'Yep, Fireman and Police.'

'Yes.'

'Right' – and he puts the phone down, turning to Sam, 'Sam, we're going to get it tomorrow.'

Acknowledgements

Particular thanks to Mr J. B. Carroll and St John the Baptist R.C. Primary School, Padiham, Lancashire.

Proceeds from this chapter are donated to ChildLine.

References

Evans, P. and Fuller, M. (1996) ' "Hello. Who am I speaking to?" communicating with pre-school children in educational research settings', *Early Years* **17**(1) 17–20.

Gillen, J. (1997) 'Couldn't put Dumpy together again: the significance of repetition and routine in young children's language development,' in Abbott, L. and Moylett, H. (eds) *Working with the Under Threes: responding to children's needs.* (Early Interactions, Vol. 2). Buckingham: Open University Press.

Hall, N. and Robinson, A. (1995) *Exploring writing and play in the early years.* London: David Fulton Publishers.

Hopper, R. (1992) *Telephone Conversation.* Bloomington, Indianapolis: Indiana University Press.

Lieven, E. (1994) 'Crosslinguistic and cross-cultural aspects of language addressed to children', in Gallaway, C. and Richards, B. J. (eds) *Input and Interaction in Language Acqusition.* Cambridge: Cambridge University Press.

Mininni, G. (1985) 'The ontogenesis of telephone interaction', *Rassegna Italiana di Linguistica Applicata* **17**(2–3), 187–97.

Moyles, J. (ed.) (1994) *The excellence of play.* Buckingham: Open University Press.

Schegloff, E. and Sacks, H. (1973) 'Opening up closings', *Semiotica* **7**, 289–327.

Spero, M. (1993) 'Use of the telephone in play therapy', in Schaefer, C. and Cangelosi, D. (eds) *Play Therapy Techniques.* Northvale, NJ: Jason Aronson.

Stenström, A.-B. (1987) 'Carry-on signals in English conversation', in Meijs, W. (ed.) *Corpus Linguistics and Beyond. Proceedings of the 7th International Conference on English Language Research of Computerized Corpora.* Amsterdam: Rodopi.

Vygotsky, L. S. (1967) 'Play and its role in the mental development of the child', *Soviet Psychology* **5**, 6–18.

Chapter 13

Choose your words carefully –
Drama, speaking and literacy
Andy Kempe

'It's the way you tell 'em!'

> A passer-by went into a shoemaker's workshop to watch the shoemaker at work, and said: 'What's that you've got there?'
>
> The shoemaker looked up from the last and said: 'Hide!'
>
> 'Hide?' repeated the passer-by, puzzled.
>
> 'Hide! Hide! A cow's outside!' said the shoemaker, irritated.
>
> The passer-by was even more puzzled. 'Why should I hide? I'm not afraid of cows…'

An ex-colleague used to tell this joke to her students to prove that they had a better knowledge of English grammar than they realised. Understanding the joke, she suggested, depended 'on an ability to distinguish nouns from verbs, adverbs from nouns and the possessive suffix 's' from the abbreviated third person singular of the verb to be' (Lyons 1990, pp. 178–9).

I'm fascinated by jokes and would not dispute that this one contains the grammatical elements my colleague identified. However, suspecting that following this joke depends on a number of other factors also, I tried it out on my own children. For my eight-year-old I paraphrased the story and animated the retelling as much as I could using different voices and exaggerated gestures. At the end he laughed loudly. 'Did you understand it, John?' I asked. 'No,' he said straightaway, 'but I liked the way you told it!'

For my eleven-year-old daughter I read the joke as it is printed above and used an animated voice but no gestures. She looked at me quizzically and pondered. 'I think I get it. Is it because there wasn't really a cow outside and the shoemaker was just … No. Oh, I don't know,' she said, and wandered off. The same strategy gained a very different reaction from her fourteen-year-old sister who gave a typically cool fourteen-year-old's response: 'Ha, Ha. Yeah, I get it. But it's not funny.'

My suspicions were being confirmed so now for the final test. This involved telling the joke to my eldest daughter's best friend – a very bright girl with particular strengths in English and a good sense of humour. In the first instance I simply read the joke to her sotto voce. She looked completely blank and admitted to having no understanding of the story at all. I tried again, this time adding voices and gestures. 'Oh right, yeah, I get it. Ha, ha,' she said. 'It's still not funny though. Can I go now?'

The point is plain enough: understanding language involves more than having an explicit or even an implicit knowledge of grammar. My simple experiment could be held to show that while an appropriate use of voice and gesture can convey the *sense* of what is being communicated, inappropriate visual and aural signs can confuse or obliterate the meaning.

However, this chapter is not intended to encourage teachers to put on funny voices and wave their arms around in order to make their classes laugh at 'naff' jokes! Rather, it is about consciously helping children recognise the different sorts of signs involved in communication and understand how they work. I will argue that drama is a particularly effective medium by which a central aim of teaching English may be addressed, that is, that pupils should: 'learn to change the way they speak and write to suit different situations, purposes and audiences' (DfEE and QCA 1999).

One more thing about the joke though, I wonder how many of my colleague's students actually knew what a shoemaker's last was? None of the young people I told the joke to knew this specialist word and none of them asked about it either. Within the context of the story one might therefore assume that it was either self-explanatory or unimportant to the overall meaning.

Talking for a purpose

When the National Curriculum for English was first being formulated the idea of incorporating speaking and listening caused much discussion. While some looked forward to seeing children being taught to 'speak properly', others were horrified by the possibility that the Orders would result in the oppression and devaluation of regional and ethnic speech codes. Others wondered why there was a need for the strand at all: most children seem to do a great deal of talking of their own volition while many teachers spent much of their working lives trying to get them to listen!

Fortunately, both the Orders for English themselves and much of the supporting material that has been made available to teachers demonstrate a recognition that speaking and listening involves sophisticated human functions and an interaction between individual and social needs. Speaking is not simply a casual activity, nor is listening a passive one. Communication is, by definition, a two-way process that involves the effective use and interpretation of a whole range of visual, aural and verbal conventions by the people communicating. As the brief analysis of the joke above demonstrates, speaking and listening is not just about speaking and listening! Moving and watching also play an important part in understanding both the nature and sense of the words spoken. Moreover, sensitivity to context that involves personal and social relationships is a vital factor in verbal communication. The capacity of deaf or blind people to engage in language based interactions is testimony to this, as is the common ability for people to capture the gist of what is being said in a foreign language they know little or nothing of.

There are a great many simple games and exercises that can illustrate to children how the visual, aural and verbal work together in the process of communication. For example, a game I call *The Window Dresser* involves the class working in pairs and imagining that they are on different sides of a plate glass window. The teacher gives one child (A) in each pair a message. The child must convey this message to their partner (B) through action alone. Messages might involve conveying a range of emotions:

Will you come to the disco with me?
Help! I've accidentally just drunk some poison!
Get out of there – the shop is on fire!
Your flies are undone.

Once B has understood the message and can repeat it aloud it is their turn to convey a new message. The exercise demands clear and economical signing by use of gesture, facial expression and mime. Pupils quickly discover that frantic arm waving and the distorted mouthing of words looks funny but ultimately fails to communicate anything. Games like this are good fun and can usefully serve as the basis for reflective discussion. However, it would be wrong to assume that the demands of the National Curriculum or the National Literacy Strategy can be met through such means. They may make a point about the complexity of communicating, but they provide little opportunity to develop skills in speaking to a purpose and learning how to extrapolate meaning from what is heard.

Effective communication results when we are able to interpret *what* it is that is being said to us. Interpretation of this *content* is aided considerably when the communicator is able to use *form*. That is, they can manipulate *how* they are saying something effectively. Drama is a particularly powerful medium of communication because of the way its form combines aspects of the visual, aural and verbal. In drama words may be used emotively, poetically and sometimes polemically. Drama can assault, tease or massage our senses and our intellect with its visual and aural imagery. It can make us laugh, cry or tremble by making what we hear contradict what we see.

Drama involves something happening to somebody somewhere. Its content gives us insights into what people might do in different situations. However, we recognise that what we see and hear in a drama is an interpretation of the real world and not the real world itself. In effective drama, the thought and selection which lies behind how content is represented helps us to understand it more fully. For the teacher, embracing the dynamics of drama thus allows 'what could be described as an "integrated" approach to teaching which seeks to keep in balance content and form' (Fleming 2000, p. 78) and in this way teachers may themselves become far more effective as communicators. What we also want though is to teach children themselves how to choose their words carefully and attend to the way they speak them. This necessarily involves making explicit what would otherwise be left as implicit. The strategy is summarised by Alan Bloch (2000, p. 11) who, in writing of his own work with drama in the primary school, notes how he tries to 'direct their attention not just to the subject of the drama, but to the very language they are using in the drama'.

Teacher in role

In his highly accessible guide to drama in the primary school, Joe Winston (2000, p. 104) asserts that:

> Classroom talk normally consists of teachers asking questions, to which they already know the answers, and the children answering them. … In drama, classroom talk is structured differently. For one thing, its hierarchical nature can be changed. The teacher may no longer be the one asking the questions; she may be silent or on the hot seat and in the firing line herself.

One way of achieving this is for the teacher to adopt a role within drama. Such a strategy can provide classes with a sharp focus for speaking and listening. The novelty implicit in experiencing their teacher working in role can be harnessed in order to heighten the children's own use and understanding of language. Sometimes this is achieved by taking a child's submission and sensitively turning it around. For example, at the start of one drama based on the disappearance of a brother and sister (a reworking of Hansel and

Gretel), I asked the class to imagine that they were experienced detectives. I invited them to chat amongst themselves about some cases in which they had been involved. Having helped the children find a 'hook' on which to base their roles, I adopted the role of a junior detective and proceeded to seek their advice on what questions to ask the missing children's father and stepmother. The way in which I carefully checked that I had understood the proposed questions made it seem as if I was deferring to their higher status roles while actively supporting the pupils' language development:

Pupil, as experienced officer: P'raps they ran away because they got told off. You could ask them if they ever told them off.

Teacher, as detective: Ah, ha! So I could ask the parents, 'How well did you and the children get on with each other? Do you often find it necessary to tell them off?'

An alternative strategy is to ask children to clarify exactly what they mean. Here again, by adopting a low status that suggests a genuine lack of understanding, the children's willingness to help someone less powerful than they feel themselves to be can encourage them to choose what to say with great care. It is always a good idea to allow the class a few moments to prepare what they want to say rather than putting them straight on the spot. This allows them to help each other formulate and check ideas resulting in fewer embarrassed silences while they try to think of what to say.

If the desired learning outcome of the drama is the development of speaking and listening skills, then it is crucial that the teacher, whether in role or not, does not say or do too much themselves. The onus needs to be on the pupils moving the drama along. This is achieved by creating a context in which what is said and done has a palpable importance. One part of a drama with a class of Year 5 children about Theseus and the Minotaur, required the children to assume the role of King Aegeus's councillors. In role as Aegeus, I used a solemn voice to relate how our enemy, King Minos, had demanded that seven maidens and seven youths be sent to Crete every nine years. In return Minos would stop the war with the people of Athens. In the first instance, each councillor was called upon simply to say 'yes' or 'no' to signal whether they agreed to the proposal. I conducted the debate through a series of short questions that demanded the councillors elaborate on their position:

'Can someone give me a reason why we should accept this offer?'
'And who will speak against this?'
'Have any of you a personal reason why we should accept?'
'Does anyone see a danger in accepting?'

By saying very little in this debate but nodding, creasing my brow and thoughtfully stroking my chin, the class realised that what they were saying was being listened to and would affect what happened next.

Modes of activity

There are three interlocking modes of activity in drama (Arts Council 1992): making, performing and responding. In the articulate classroom of the primary school one would certainly expect to see children engaging in all three. Further examples from the Theseus drama, which was video recorded, illustrate how engagement with making, performing and responding may be facilitated.

For example, I invited the class to imagine King Minos' palace at Knossos. After brainstorming ideas as a whole class regarding what the palace of such a powerful King might have looked like, the children worked in pairs. The exercise, which needs to be carefully explained and demonstrated by the teacher, involves one child keeping their eyes closed while the other leads them around the palace describing the opulent setting. The children with their shut eyes should constantly ask their sighted partner questions: 'How big is it?' 'What colour?' 'What's the floor like?' It is extraordinary how this exercise can help children create a clear mental image of a place. The rich descriptions that result can generate powerful creative writing. In this case, however, I drew on the children's ideas about the palace and narrated how a group of ambassadors from Athens visited Minos in order to try and persuade him to stop the war.

Teacher:	What impression do we, as a court, want to give these ambassadors from Athens? What do we want them to think about us?
Child 1:	That we are stronger than them.
Child 2:	That we are better than them.
Child 3:	That we're tough.
Child 4:	We're posh. ...
Child 5:	... and really rich.
Teacher:	Then show me how you are going to impress them.

The talk here is in the realm of making drama. There is no need for a teacher to go 'over the top' in such role play; rather, the role is subtly signalled through the language by shifting from past to present tense and changing the pronouns. Having established an idea of place and an appropriate atmosphere, further decisions were quickly made regarding what characters would be present in Minos' throne room: soldiers, advisers, scribes, servants, etc. The attitudes of these characters towards the ambassadors were revealed by inviting them to speak their thoughts aloud as they waited for the ambassadors. Meanwhile, another group of children had been planning how to present the Athenians' case to the court. Having set the scene, it was time to perform it:

Teacher:	(adopting role by ostentatiously sitting on the 'throne', puffing his chest out and gesturing with a wave of his hand) 'Show them in.' Two pupils mime opening a pair of huge, imagined doors. Four ambassadors enter. They pull comic faces to denote that the situation looks frightening. Laughter.
Teacher:	(out of role) 'Uh, uh – serious, serious.' The class gather themselves. The ambassadors walk slowly between the courtiers who stare and snigger at them. They stop before the king and courtiers. Three kneel and keep bowing while one steps forward and speaks.
Ambassador:	'On behalf of all of us I'd like to try and call off this war. It wasn't our fault that your son was killed. It was really his own choice. Um ... it was his choice about whether to go and try and kill the bull or not because ...' (turning to others) 'What else?' (one shrugs, another mouths something) 'Yes, and it's not worth it really. Too many of us, too many of your people and our people are getting killed for nothing.' (Silence)
Teacher (as Minos):	'My son is lying dead outside your city walls. You don't seem to be offering us anything at all to pay for his death.' (Silence) The spokesperson looks genuinely worried. The courtiers have

stopped sniggering. They are waiting for the ambassador's answer. Or is it that this little girl's classmates are waiting to see what she will do?

There is an electricity about scenes such as this generated by the teacher deliberately challenging the pupils. If may seem intimidating – that's because it is! So long as the teacher acts with restraint and watches very carefully for any sign that the children have had enough, there is a vicarious pleasure to be had in the experience. Here is the next part of the lesson:

Teacher: (breaking out of role by completely relaxing in the chair, smiling, making eye contact with as many children in the class as possible and signalling with his hands that they may all sit down) 'Wow! That was something wasn't it? What was it like for you Annabel?'
Annabel: 'It was funny.'
Teacher: (incredulous) 'Funny? Why?'
Annabel: 'Because we'd decided what we were going to say and then you made it more difficult and we didn't know what to do.'
Teacher: 'Ah. Was it just me, or do you think that the rest of the group managed to show that they were stronger and more powerful than you?'
Annabel: 'I don't know really – I didn't look at them!'
Girl 2:   'They looked pretty posh!'
Teacher: 'Posh?'
Girl 3:   'Scary.'
Teacher: 'So it worked then? Can any of you (gesturing to the courtiers) suggest what the ambassadors might have done to make a better impression on us?'

The QCA guidance *Teaching Speaking and Listening in Key Stages 1 and 2* (1999) suggests an appropriate focus for drama would be: 'enacting a ceremony, e.g. *a coronation or wedding, using speech and silence.* Consider how meaning and impact are expressed by movement, gesture, etc.'. In the Theseus drama the children were guided through the processes of making and performing a ceremony in which movement, gesture, eye contact, silence and tone certainly had meaning and impact. Through reflection, the scene came to serve as a basis for other groups of ambassadors to discuss and try out different techniques designed to persuade Minos to stop the war.

Later in the same drama, having been shown some examples of classical paintings depicting scenes from other myths, the children were asked to imagine how a Renaissance painter might have depicted the scene in which Theseus returns from the labyrinth triumphantly holding the head of the Minotaur. The task stimulated considerable discussion around style, genre and character. How would Theseus' fellow Athenians react to his victory? Would they waste time showing their adulation, or would they just want to escape? More interesting still was the debate surrounding where to put Ariadne in the picture. Should she look adoringly up at Theseus or nervously at the door? Creating a visually dramatic image became an exploration of art history and quite a heated debate about representations of gender followed!

Context and consequence

Drama provides a rich context in which children may hone their ability to speak to suit different situations, purposes and audiences because the consequences of what is spoken and done within the bounds of the dramatic narrative resonate with real life concerns: 'it is a way of considering possibilities, of making worlds' (Meek 1990 p. 149).

De-contextualised exercises and games, while relating to and drawing on different dynamics of drama, ultimately fail to offer children the rich learning experiences that result from carefully planned dramatic explorations of a narrative. Drama works best when it is fun. However, ensuring that it is fun is a serious business. Consider what sort of dramas you personally enjoy and why, and perhaps you will realise that the characters and issues at the heart of dramatic narratives need not necessarily be explored in dark, dismal and depressing ways. Winston and Tandy (1998) are among many prac-titioners and commentators to promote the potential of folk-tales, myths and legends as the bases for exciting dramas while the Shakespeare in Schools project amply illustrates the wealth of themes and ideas to be found in Shakespeare's work. The durability of such tales and characters rests on their capacity to relate to wide audiences across time and distance. Film versions reworking traditional tales of Robin Hood and King Arthur pop up every few years. Innumerable romantic dramas can be identified with Cinderella and Rapunzel, and Disney's retelling of 'Hamlet', that is, 'The Lion King', is, as I write, the hottest show in London's West End.

Part of the appeal of these narratives is the way they address moral questions. Have you ever considered how the most interesting fictional characters are the ones who are in some way deeply flawed? Heroes and heroines who are practically perfect in every way can, like Tony Ross's *Super Dooper Jezebel* (1988), be a bit of a bore and a turn off, whereas villains from Dennis the Menace to Hannibal Lecter seem far more engaging. This is because they cause us to question our own moral standpoint. In drama children's feelings are engaged in a positive way by arousing concern for an individual, or a nega-tive way 'by arousing their mistrust or their indignation. In both cases, children are being encouraged to care for their fellow human beings, for the difficult situations they find themselves in and for the consequences of their actions, whether good or bad' (Winston 2000, p. 105).

Talking, listening and literacy

So far in this chapter I have argued that effective spoken communication is dependent on both the choice of words and the aural and visual manner in which they are delivered. Children's ability to recognise this and develop their skill in communicating effectively can be enhanced by the creation of a dramatic context in which the rela-tionship between form and content is made explicit and is seen to have consequences that matter. During drama, children feel an investment in the characters and the outcome of the unfolding narrative. This dynamic can generate focused and purposeful talk and also promote acute listening. For example, in another part of the Theseus drama the class were asked to imagine that they were the Athenian youths imprisoned in a cell adjacent to the labyrinth. In role as Ariadne, I knocked gently at an imagined door and said that I wanted to speak to Theseus about my plan to help them escape. Out of role, I pointed out that all the Athenians had to judge whether Ariadne was genuine or trick-ing them with the sound of her voice and what she actually said. The class discussed this for a while then ask to play they scene again on the grounds that they need to listen more attentively!

Context makes the meaning matter. Such a powerful motivator for speaking and listening can also be harnessed to encourage children to write. In another section of the Theseus drama I used narration and 'thought tracking' to build tension in the scene in which seven youths and seven maidens would be chosen by King Aegeus to be sacrificed to the Minotaur. Having written their names on a slip of paper and placed them in a special 'choosing urn', the children were given another slip of paper and asked to write down as quickly as possible how they were feeling about the possibility of their name being drawn out. The following example, written in just a few minutes, amply demonstrates the way drama can generate a pressing reason to write.

> I hope they don't choose me. Perhaps I should tear up the ticket with my name on, then they won't choose me. I'll move away. I've got to move away. Maybe I should just think happy thoughts because this might be the last time I'm happy. Please don't choose me …

Young people need to grow in their understanding of language use – both spoken and written – and particularly in their ability to interpret meaning within social contexts. Drama can provide a most supportive means of learning through imagined experience. One way of ending this chapter would be to issue a rallying call to use drama as the panacea for current concerns about children's standards of behaviour and literacy. Another would be to further cite the National Curriculum, QCA, OFSTED, etc., by way of threatening teachers to use drama or else! But I think I'll choose my words carefully: if you haven't tried using drama already, try it. If you have and it's worked, develop it.

References

Arts Council of Great Britain (1992) *Drama in Schools*. London: Arts Council of Great Britain.

Bloch, A. (2000) 'Reading the stories we construct together', in Ackroyd, J. *Literacy Alive!* London: Hodder & Stoughton.

DfEE and QCA (1999) *The National Curriculum*. London: DfEE and QCA.

Fleming, M. (2000) 'A highwayman comes riding', in Ackroyd, J. *Literacy Alive!* London: Hodder & Stoughton.

Lyons, H. (1990) 'What Katy knows about language', in Carter, R. (ed.) *Knowledge about Language and the Curriculum*. London: Hodder & Stoughton.

Meek, M. (1990) 'What do we know about reading that helps us teach?', in Carter, R. (ed.) *Knowledge about Language and the Curriculum*. London: Hodder & Stoughton.

Ross, T. (1988) *Super Dooper Jezebel*. London: Anderson Press.

QCA (1999) *Teaching Speaking and Listening in Key stages 1 and 2*. London: QCA.

Winston, J. (2000) *Drama, Literacy and Moral Education 5–11*. London: David Fulton Publishers.

Winston, J. and Tandy, M. (1998) *Beginning Drama 4–11*. London: David Fulton Publishers.

Chapter 14

Crick Crack Chin my Story's in – Stories and storytelling

Teresa Grainger

Once a man, lost in the jungle for many days, caught a fever that gripped his frame so tenaciously that he grew weak and frail. He struggled feebly through the undergrowth in an almost unconscious state, until at last he collapsed. Later, it seemed to him the face of a great lion loomed over him, but then it disappeared. The lion returned however and with its huge head inclined over the man, it let a few drops of water trickle into his mouth. Every day the king of beasts brought the man water and later left pieces of fruit beside him. Eventually, the man found he could stand again, and while the lion was away he found his way back to his village.

'We thought you were dead,' cried his friends. 'Whatever happened?'

'A lion attacked me,' he replied, 'but I killed it with my bare hands. It has taken me a long time to recover.'

Three months later, the man once again adventuring in the jungle came across the lion. Silently they stared into each other's eyes. 'Take your knife,' commanded the lion, 'and cut my head.' The man did as he was bid, until blood trickled down into the lion's thick mane. The man dropped his weapon and walked slowly away.

A further three months passed and the man met the king of beasts again. 'Look at me.' demanded the lion, 'What do you see?'

'The wound on your head has healed.'

'Yes,' replied the lion, 'but the wound inside me will never heal.'

My tale I have told it, in your heart now you may hold it.

Stories and storytelling have always been used to teach about the human condition, and continue to offer teachers a rich cornucopia of delight with personal, oral, traditional and literary tales just waiting to be told. Children deserve to experience the energising nature of storytelling, the rhythms, tunes and truths of tales told and retold. Their spoken confidence and competence, their power over written narrative and their reading will all benefit if sustained opportunities to share tales of all kinds are offered. In such contexts, the classroom becomes a community of storytellers who create, investigate, shape, share, value and learn from their own and others' stories.

> Storytelling is the direct and shared communication of something true about being alive. It is not only the story, but a combination of a living storyteller, situation, sound and rhythm of voice, silence, gesture, facial expressions, and response of listeners that makes it potent.
>
> (Simms 1982)

This chapter seeks to examine the significance of children's engagement in stories and storytelling, to explore support strategies for the teller, the tale and the told and to highlight the contribution that oral storytelling can make to learning in language and literacy.

Storytelling: a learning tradition

In preliterate societies, storytelling was a highly significant form of education and even in today's technological age it remains an accessible intellectual resource. The children we teach are crammed with anecdotes, hopes, warnings, explanations, jokes, family stories, reminiscences, televisual tales and tales read, heard and created which are relayed in countless conversations and playful contexts. Their humanity is expressed in the anecdotes and stories they choose to tell one another in the street, the playground, the classroom, at home and on the phone. Through telling stories, humans make sense of lived and vicarious experiences and structure their identity, since, as Hardy (1977) has argued, narrative is a primary act of mind, a mode of thinking and searching for understanding. Rosen (1988) has called it an 'irrepressible genre', a primary cognitive instrument which enables us to comprehend what events mean to us, through our inner and outer storytelling (Bruner 1986, Rosen 1984, Clandinin and Connelly 1990). In addition to its role in cognition, a correlation between early experience of story and later educational achievement has been found (Wells 1987), and the impact of young children hearing stories is widely recognised (Dombey 1988, Dickinson 1995). Through hearing stories, children learn about the features and organisation of language, and begin to assimilate and understand the more abstract mode of representing experience through writing (Wells 1987, Olson 1984).

Young children's conception of story, and how to tell a story is not only based upon the stories they have heard but also on the games they have played, the countless conversations they have taken part in, and the TV and video they have watched (Anderson and Hilton 1997). Through hearing stories and telling tales, their awareness of story, character and plot is gradually expanded into aspects of linguistic style, use of narrative technique and the syntax necessary for complex thinking (Fox 1993). Although it is undoubtedly true that children's preschool experience and cultural use of story differs (Brice-Heath 1983, Minns 1990), storytelling is a general language habit, and thinking through story remains a universal human competence, which can be developed and refined in school (Egan 1988, Bage 1999). 'We need to learn strategies of narration when we are very young in order to grasp that we can become our own narrators, the storytellers of our lives' (Zipes 1995).

Stories play a critical role in self-creation as well as self-discovery, so no one need be a prisoner of their own autobiography, at least from a constructivist viewpoint. Furthermore, if we are to work *with children* in our classrooms, and not merely deliver prescribed curricula to *pupils*, then opportunities to value their own lives, their stories and cultural experience need to be created and built upon in the classroom. Narrative plays an important part in both cognitive and emotional development and needs to be recognised more fully as a tool for learning, right across the primary years. Narrative thought is supported not only by literature based classrooms, but by a range of classroom contexts such as play, drama and storytelling, all of which contribute effectively and affectively to children's oral and literate development, building their sense of self and expanding their imaginative capacity. When a storytelling ethos is established and the oral and literary traditions are both valued, then the National Curriculum (DfEE 1999) requirement to integrate the three language modes can be fully realised. But in order to achieve this successfully, the tale, the teller and the told, must all work in harmony (Colwell 1991, Medlicott 1989).

The tales

Traditional tales, myths, legends and fables from many cultures are endorsed by both *The National Curriculum* (1999) and the *National Literacy Strategy: Framework for Teaching* (NLSF) (DfEE 1998), and many of these lend themselves to oral storytelling, dramatic investigation and joint performance. Such tales are identified as a generic focus for literacy work in every year group, except Year 4/6 when they can easily be encompassed within 'stories which raise issues' or in order to revisit a genre explored earlier. Personal stories are also recognised as central within the NLSF, and are given a focus in each autumn term. Although, in reality they will permeate throughout the year, as children interweave elements of their lives into their written stories (Bearne 1998) and make life to text and text to life connections in their reading (Meek 1990).

Short evocative stories and personal anecdotes work wonders if the teller is in tune with the tale's layers of meaning, and recognises their own desire to share that particular story. Well-known tales, or parodies of them, maybe too frequently visited, given the breadth of multicultural literature available in tapes and books (see Grainger 1997 for a recommended list), although less experienced tellers may prefer to share personal tales which create an instant rapport. There is no doubt that a teller's enthusiasm for a tale is infectious, allowing the story to be creatively 'sung' into existence, inspiring commitment and response. 'I love telling The Master Thief, the ending is just amazing,' ten-year-old Rosie declared. 'You can see the penny beginning to drop as you speak.' In preparing to tell the tale to others, children can draw upon a range of comprehension strategies to recall the story shape, which can be modelled by the teacher in shared reading and used in independent work. These include:

- *The Three Seeds of Story:* This indicates the beginning, middle and end of the tale, pictures are drawn to deconstruct a tale (or plan a new one), and are then watered by the storyteller's words in their retelling.
- *The Story Mountain:* This reflects the trajectory of the story and is particularly useful for climactic stories. Symbols, pictures or words which represent key events in the tale are depicted on the mountain range.
- *A Skeletal Summary:* This constitutes a keyword summary to highlight the features and aid recall. Significant phrases from the story can be included. For example:
Man–lost/ill
Lion–water/fruit
Man–better/return
LIED
Man–lion 'cut my head'
Lion–man 'wound has healed.'
Wound inside FOREVER (Shaun, aged 8)

In using such strategies to recall the overall sequence of events, the storyteller becomes better acquainted with the tale: however tales are not recalled as a series of structural moves alone, but as a story inhabited by living characters. Strategies to understand these include emotions maps or graphs, sociograms and drama conventions, e.g. role play, hot seating or interior monologues. Such activities can prompt retelling from a particular character's perspective and should allow time to dwell within the tale, exploring it from the inside out. Classroom drama in particular can give rise to further storytelling while living imaginatively within the frame of the overarching narrative (Grainger and Cremin 2000).

The teller

Humans are natural tale tellers, although not everyone has the confidence to tell to an audience. Teachers can lean on the everyday nature of narrative, their experience of life and literature and their often unrecognised imaginative capacity. Teachers' voices, their bodies and emotional response are underrated yet vital resources in the primary classroom, as Graham (1999) has shown in relation to struggling boy readers. The experience of storytelling and the overt use of creative voice play, silence, pace, gesture and body movement, can play a significant role in expanding teachers and children's vocal/physical repertoires, and release their creative energy through emotional involvement with the tale and the told.

Practice in telling any tale is vital to 'own' and shape the story, to experience its rhythms, flavour, feel and temperature. In voicing even one part of a tale in our own words, we make spontaneous choices about vocabulary, style, language and imagery and inhabit the story we are recreating. All the storyboards, maps, or timelines in the world can never replace the importance of orally retelling and reshaping stories, releasing them from the mind to explore their meanings and voice their truths. There are many ways to organise partial retellings, which can take place as a precursor to shared writing or in independent work. These can focus on character, setting, plot, language or the features of the genre as appropriate, and include:

- *Retelling in teller and listener pairs:* Following a story, pairs take it in turns to retell part of the tale. The teacher can revisit a section to re-voice the tale's tune and then pairs continue, swapping roles at the beat of a tambourine.
- *Creating a significant visual picture:* Pairs share a favourite, striking, bizarre, thought-provoking visual from the tale. Each child retells only one section, starting just before and finishing just after the visual picture in their mind's eye. This prompts detail and depth and avoids the relentless push of narrative action.
- *Retelling extracts from story dice:* These are made with symbols representing tales from the class' repertoire. In groups, a number dice is thrown, when a six emerges, the story dice is thrown and an extract from the tale depicted.
- *Creating endings through rainbow groupings:* The teacher tells only part of the tale and challenges groups to generate ideas to finish it. Rainbow regrouping enables each child to retell their group's agreed ending and highlights diversity as well as common themes.

If the tape recorder is used, oral drafting of tales becomes possible and storytelling conferences can also be established, with the class creating a corporate list of storytelling conventions and using these to comment upon their own and others' retellings. Their reflective responses could focus upon the teller's use of voice, gesture or dialect, any strong images created, the appropriacy of words chosen and the tenor and feel of the tale. Conferences constitute rich material for plenary sessions in mini blocks on traditional tales or personal stories, particularly when children are working towards a storytelling event of some form.

The told

Storytelling is a social process, an interactive art form which creates a common bond between the teller and the told. The immediacy and intimacy of the situation creates a shared experience, which while it is only temporary, is both evocative and powerful, teasing out the imaginative and linguistic potential of all involved. Captured by the teller's inflection, pause and pace, the audience is drawn into the narrative and become both spectators and participants on the journey, actively creating the tale in their own imaginations and prompting the storyteller to take their interests into account. As Hugh Lupton, the storyteller, observes, the teller has to straddle two worlds.

> One foot is in the place where the story is being told, holding the attention of the listeners; the other foot is in the place where the story happens. ... His outer eye looks towards his audience, his inner eye searches out the story, and the words on his tongue relay the inner world to the outer.   (Lupton 2000)

Children can develop this capacity and grow in confidence from the pleasure and satisfaction gained through each successful storytelling encounter. 'They *really* listened to me.' Abby (aged 9) exclaimed excitedly. 'They looked afraid, almost scared. It was like we were all there together, watching her fall, wondering what would happen. I knew, but I made them wait ...' Telling stories often leads to a time of reflection and response in which the class can explore the meanings and values in the story, through discussion, art, drama, dance, reading or writing. Open-ended activities, built upon the common bond of the told tale, engender thoughtful comprehension and considerably enrich understanding: since the children are involved in the tale from the outset, their responses are built upon this shared emotive and felt experience.

Storytelling: language and literacy learning

Oral stories, whether personal or traditional, are useful resources for the literacy hour since they provoke children's curiosity and speak to their feelings, evoking identification, response and engagement. When a written text is available, comparisons between the spoken and written versions may be made, when one is not, key features and memorable phrases may still be scribed for sentence and word level work. Blocked units of work on tales can involve all the language modes as well as drama, music, citizenship and art and need to be well-resourced with quality collections and picture book versions, not merely old and tired copies of folk and fairy tales. Such units can focus on myths, legends, folk-tales, fables, family stories, local tales or community histories and may usefully work towards a storytelling afternoon, the production of story tapes or an anthology of retold tales. Professional storytellers offer a lot to such work (e.g. the TASTE (Teaching as Storytelling) Project, Bage 2000, Zipes 1995), especially if their example encourages teachers, children, parents and the community to tell tales, value others' stories and recognise that storytelling does more than contribute to raised standards in language and literacy.

Developing speaking and listening

Storytelling offers children the chance to take 'long turns' in the classroom, to be listened to and given the creative space to develop their communicative competence. In telling, hearing and reflecting upon told tales, children develop their understanding of how spoken language works; how pause and pace, humour and irony, inflection and emphasis can be used for effect, why certain words or phrases retain their impact, and how to draw listeners in and hold their attention. Children can also learn about the structures and conventions of oral narrative, about standard and non-standard English, colloquialisms, idioms and the differences between oral and written versions (Howe and Johnson 1992). Their confidence, oral competence, memory, vocabulary and sense of self can also be positively influenced as they tell tales which entertain others, share cultural understandings, bridge gaps and gain perspective on their own lives.

Yet teachers too often demand written exposition of personal stories, effectively short changing oral tales on the grounds of time and their transient nature. But autobiography matters and personal anecdotes must be recognised as part of the educational agenda. Darren, a quiet youngster, gained tremendous kudos and confidence through his mother's taped retelling of ten sausages igniting and her son's valiant attempt to rescue the dog and save the day! Her story became so well known in school that eventually she joined us to tell it in person. Her increased involvement undoubtedly affected Darren, who seemed 'released' by the storytelling work, and began to value his life stories, reinterpret his sense of self and volunteer his views. Personal stories must be voiced and can be triggered in a number of ways including:

- the teacher/classroom assistant/visitor telling their own tales and anecdotes;
- photographs of events, postcards of places visited;
- personal objects which prompt memories;
- literature which reminds us of events/people/occasions;
- class/personal timelines, e.g. the last term at school;
- family stories captured on tape.

Retelling traditional tales similarly fosters oral development, experimentation and imitation as Kieron's retold extract from the tale *The Very Mean King* indicates.

> 'Now this mean King never smiled, not once. Never laughed, not ever. Never joked, never, never, ever. But he did stamp – "Stamp-Stamp-Stamp" and he did shout – "Get On With Your Work!" and he did snarl – "Snarl, Hiss, Snarl". He hated everyone and he made a law so no one would laugh or smile or be happy. It was the most miserable place to live. All day the people had to work hard in his fields and everyday he would shout and snarl at them; "Get On With Your Work! – Snarl, Hiss, Snarl – Get On With Your Work! – Stamp, Stamp, Stamp." But what the King didn't know was that a magic sparrow from heaven was watching him and she felt sorry for the sad people so ...'

This partial printed record cannot convey Kieron's verve, commitment or pleasure in telling his tale. His eyes were alight, and his gestures free as he played with the devices of the oral tradition and explored the latent possibilities in his voice. His affective involvement in the story captured his Year 3 audience, grouped as they were around his storyteller's chair. They hung on his every word and followed his every gesture, demanding to know afterwards if it was true and had he really spoken to the magic sparrow himself? In both the telling and the interchange that followed, Kieron was exercising considerable power over language and exhibiting his creative capacity which would have been much more difficult for him to demonstrate in writing. While it was structurally similar to the Kenyan tale he had read in *The Big Wide Mouthed Toad Frog and Other Stories* (Medlicott 1996), Kieron had made the tale his own. He used his own words and emphatic actions to denote the king's behaviour and added his own relationship to the sparrow, which he told us visited him often and had other stories to tell. 'I wish the magic sparrow would come and visit me!' Alisdair declared. Kieron's use of story language, cohesive devices, rhythm, repetition and changes in pace and volume indicate his developing awareness of how such stories work and his growing confidence as a tale teller. All children deserve such opportunities.

Developing writing and reading

Once the tale has been told, owned, shaped and shared on the tongue, then the act of writing becomes a way of recording, a chance to reshape it still further. Through direct teaching and considerable experience in telling traditional tales with their clear structures, memorable characters, repetitive and figurative language and archetypal issues, children can come to use these features in their own written work. But merely isolating these in shared reading and including them in shared writing, without involving the spoken word extensively and regularly will not produce lasting effects. Retelling enables the writer to lean on the given framework of events and frees them to work on the emotional or physical landscape of the tale or the nature and motives of the characters. Such retelling can be very empowering as Emily's writing from *The Seven Standing Stories of Phloubinec* shows.

> As the clock struck twelve all the laws of nature changed and every animal created stopped still. Bernez saw a deer frozen in its tracks and a bat hanging in the sky. He was amazed. Then the great stones began to move, pulling themselves out of their sockets and lumbering down to the water to drink. At first Bernez too stood still, holding tightly to his four-leaved clover, he watched with wide eyes. Then he hurried to the hole left by the largest stone. He looked down and saw a layer of dreams before him. There were jewels shining in the moonlight, jewels that would let him marry Madeleine at last. Surely, he thought, her father would say yes now. There were gold and silver ingots too, money to pay for his mother to see a doctor, money to mend her leg and help her walk again. In a daze Bernez smiled to himself as he stared at the treasure. 'Bernez' shrieked the beggar beside him, 'Hurry up, get down there, and pass it all up to me …'

In the original telling of the tale, this part had been passed over, the teacher merely noted that Bernez saw 'treasure upon treasure' in the void beneath the largest stone. In the follow-up work, Emily had collaboratively retold the whole tale from Bernez' perspective. In this group context she had voiced, heard and felt Bernez' hopes and desires, his unrequited love for the Squire's daughter and his concern for his mother. It would seem that the experience of telling gave her an insight into his character, so that in narrating this she is able to reflect Bernez' thoughts and feelings and prefigure the tale to come.

Through regular opportunities to tell tales and reflect upon them, children come to internalise story structures (e.g. problem – resolution, cumulative tales) as well as use a broader and more effective vocabulary. The rich descriptions, patterns, images, symbols and memorable language of traditional tales can be tacitly transferred into their writing as the following extracts indicate. These Year 2 writers creating their own tales used stylistic devices borrowed from the oral tradition:

> Have you ever worried about being fat? Well this story is about a girl who …

> … and you can be sure that Max never touched that piece of paper again!

> 'Crack, Crack!' went the whip, 'Crack, Crack!' Can you hear it? 'Crack, Crack!'

> In a time before our time began there lived a tiny ant, and a very tiny ant he was to be sure.

> And as it was then, so it is now. Look around you, there are good and bad people everywhere.

Their narrative writing reflected other resonances of the tales they had told: in the structures, characters, repetitive refrains and vocabulary as well as in their sense of audience and awareness of ways to draw in the reader. Narrative writing, authorial voice and style can all be enriched through storytelling, which enables children to hear and taste the colour and drama in the words they have chosen.

Storytelling and reading also feed off one another, for in searching for 'unknown' tales to tell, children are prompted to widen their reading in this genre and develop their understanding of the features of story. Through interpreting the teller's gestures, expression and intonation they practise inference and deduction and even the most reluctant reader is provoked to picture, predict and ponder on the tale. In addition, teachers' narrative voices that explore their full range, tone, volume and emotional tenor offer a powerful model for fluent reading, likewise the developing voice of the child storyteller can significantly influence their expressive reading.

Conclusion

The power and potency of storytelling can only be harnessed in the classroom if teachers themselves are prepared to develop their own latent oral narrative skills (Grugeon *et al.* 1998) as well as provide opportunities for the children. A creative activity, it enables tellers to engage in the time honoured tradition of revisiting and recreating their common culture, developing their verbal artistry and extending their linguistic competence. As teachers we must seek to ensure that storytelling is not perceived as just a passing activity, undertaken to respond to an attainment target or to prepare for writing, nor simply an occasional treat to be experienced when funds allow. It is a way of learning, reflecting and understanding, which can connect home and school, develop the imagination, extend language and literacy, and motivate, energise and delight both teachers and children alike.

Crick Crack Snout My Tale is Out

References

Anderson, H. and Hilton, M. (1997) 'Speaking subjects: the development of a conceptual framework for the teaching and learning of speaking and listening', *English in Education* **31**(1) (NATE).

Bage, G. (1999) *Narrative Matters: Teaching and Learning History Through Story.* London: Falmer Press.

Bage, G. (2000) 'Developing teaching as storytelling', in Hodges, C., Drummond, G. and Styles, M. *Tales, Tellers and Texts.* London: Cassell.

Bearne, E. (1998) 'Where do stories come from?' in Styles, M., Bearne, E. and Watson, V. *The Prose and the Passion.* London: Cassell.

Brice Heath, S. (1983) *Ways with Words: Language, Life and Work in Communities and Classrooms.* Cambridge: Cambridge University Press.

Bruner, J. (1986) *Actual Minds, Possible Worlds.* Cambridge, Mass.: Harvard University Press.

Clandinin, D. and Connelly, F. (1990) 'Narrative, experience and the study of the curriculum', *Cambridge Journal of Education* **20**(3).

Colwell, E. (1991) *Storytelling.* Stroud: Thimble Press.

DfEE (1998) *The National Literacy Strategy: Framework for Teaching.* London: DfEE.

DfEE (1999) *The National Curriculum*. London: DfEE.

Dickinson, T. (1995) *Bridges to Literacy: Children, Families and Schools*. Oxford: Blackwell.

Dombey, H. (1988) 'Partners in the telling', in Meek, M. and Mills, C. *Language and Literacy in the Primary School*. London: Falmer Press.

Egan, K. (1988) *Teaching as Storytelling*. London: Routledge.

Fox, C. (1993) *At the Very Edge of the Forest: The Influence of Literature on Storytelling by Children*. London: Cassell.

Graham, L. (1999) 'Changing practice through reflection: The Key Stage 2 Reading Project, Croydon', *Reading* **33**(3).

Grainger, T. (1997) *Traditional Storytelling in the Primary Classroom*. Warwickshire: Scholastic.

Grainger, T. and Cremin, M. (2000) *Resourcing Drama 5–8*, Loughborough: NATE.

Grugeon, E., Hubbard, L., Smith, C. and Dawes, L. (1998) *Teaching Speaking and Listening in the Primary School*. London: David Fulton Publishers.

Hardy, B. (1977) 'Towards a poetics of fiction: an approach through narrative', in Meek, M., Warlow, A., and Barton, G. (eds) *The Cool Web*. London: The Bodley Head.

Howe, A. and Johnson, J. (1992) *Common Bonds: Storytelling in the Classroom*. London: Hodder & Stoughton.

Lupton, H. (2000) 'Betsy Whyte and the Dreaming', in Hodges, C., Drummond, G. and Styles, M. *Tales, Tellers and Texts*. London: Cassell.

Medlicott, M. (ed.) (1989) *By Word of Mouth: The Revival Of Storytelling*. London: Channel 4 Broadside Publications.

Medlicott, M. (ed.) (1996) *The Big Wide Mouthed Toad Frog and Other Stories*. London: Kingfisher.

Meek, M. (1990) *On Being Literate*. London: The Bodley Head.

Minns, H. (1990) *Read it to Me Now*. London: Virago.

Olson, D. (1984) 'See! Jumping! Some oral antecedents of literacy', in Goelman, H., Oberg, A. and Smith, F. (eds) *Awakening To Literacy*. Portsmouth: Heinemann.

Rosen, H. (1984) *Stories and Meanings*. Sheffield: NATE.

Rosen, H. (1988) 'The irrepressible genre', in Maclure, M., Phillips, T. and Wilkinson, A. *Oracy Matters*. Milton Keynes: Open University Press.

Simms, L. (1982) 'Storytelling, children and imagination', *The Yarnspinner* **6**(2) Heinemann.

Wells, G. (1987) *The Meaning Makers*. London: Hodder & Stoughton.

Zipes, J. (1995) *Creative Storytelling: Building Community, Changing Lives*. London: Routledge.

Chapter 15

'Jessica and Jordan meet an alien' – Creating a story in a multilingual classroom

Jackie Kirk

The background to the story

'When can we write part two of the Jessica and Jordan story?' This question was asked as soon as I walked into a third grade classroom after the long summer break. It convinced me of the significance of this story for a certain class of second grade students in a Montreal elementary school and caused me to reflect anew on the project I had been involved in with them the previous school year. *Jessica and Jordan meet an alien* had been written during the Spring of the last school year as part of a whole-class storying project. The class teacher and I had been working together on a regular basis over the year, developing an innovative language arts programme that would motivate the students and provide opportunities for them to be successful, 'authentic' readers, writers and story 'knowers'.

As a professional development consultant with the school, I had been working with different teachers in different ways, responding to their individual and class needs. My one day a week was spent meeting with teachers to plan and review projects as well as joining in with team-teaching and generally supporting in-class activities. The school's student population reflects the cultural and linguistic make-up of the community in which it is situated, and the second grade class was a microcosm of the school as a whole. Over 70 per cent of the school's students speak a first language other than English or French, with Tamil being the most commonly spoken (about 25 per cent of the students are Tamils of Sri Lankan origin), closely followed by Punjabi, Gujurati, Bengali and Urdu. There are also smaller numbers of students speaking Greek, Chinese, Twi, Poshto and other languages.

The work I describe in Room 17 was a part of a new 'Storying in many tongues' project which was slowly taking off in the school. As a school community, we were aware of the rich language and cultural resources the students possess in their first languages and we wanted to find ways of connecting with and drawing on these to support their learning in English. We started to experiment with the gradual integration of the students' home languages into some language arts and other activities, into the classroom in general and into the school as a whole. This idea took different forms in different classes, with different teachers. It involved students, their parents, community members and students from our local secondary school to which most of the students would go. The main objectives of the project are at the core of the school's mission:

- to stimulate interest in and appreciation of different languages;
- to promote a positive model of bilingualism;
- to find ways of building on and developing the linguistic and cultural experiences of the students in all languages in ways that will create success for them in school.

'Storying in many tongues' addressed all three of the objectives of the school development plan in a concrete and original way. It also enabled staff to develop the literacy skills and the self-esteem of all students and to develop stronger links between the school, parents and the community.

An appreciation of the strong connections between oracy and literacy was at the heart of the work. So was the conviction that school must provide a safe climate in which individuals are encouraged to express themselves, can feel valued and can develop confidence and self-esteem. Individual expression of ideas generally happens most often, most spontaneously and most easily through talk. In such a multilingual environment, concern for talk cannot be limited to the English language, and especially not if our intention is to value, and seek to build on, learning through talk outside the classroom walls.

At the beginning of the project, a number of commercially produced bilingual children's story-books, with text in both English and one of the home languages, provided an initial stimulus. These were shared in class and taken home to read with parents and family. Other related activities soon developed. Parents and resource staff started working together to prepare and tell other stories simultaneously in two languages in class. These stories were often their own. Grade 6 students also became storytellers, reading and telling stories in their own languages. The following description of the storying project in the second grade class and some of the subsequent related activities, seeks to highlight the importance of talk in student learning, and to provide an example of how an inclusive concept of talk – talk in 'many tongues' – can be effectively and enjoyably practised in an English-medium classroom.

Who are Jessica and Jordan?

Jessica and Jordan are the child protagonists of a story written by the second grade class. Their class teacher, Meta, and I were keen to follow-up a couple of bilingual storytelling sessions her students had greatly enjoyed. Through discussion, we decided on a class storying project, one that would be flexible in design, depending very much on the interest of the students. We were also keen to use the project to develop the skills of the students in working cooperatively in groups and in pairs. The stimulus for our story were two string puppets, introduced simply as characters with no story; it was going to be up to the group to create one for them. As soon as these puppets appeared, the students were hooked and ideas for their story were soon flying backwards and forwards across the class! Modelling a team-effort to the students, Meta and I managed to structure the enthusiasm a little, encouraging the students to use their existing knowledge of stories to build up a logical sequence of events and consequences. I animated the lively discussion while Meta wrote out the emerging story on large sheets of paper. Inevitably some students spoke up more than others, but with some encouragement, quieter students also contributed ideas and suggested wording. Everyone took part in crucial votes on certain aspects of the story development. In later reflection, and as I write now, I realise the potential for asking many more questions about the process: Who were the main contributors to the story? Which children had most influence on the direction the story took? Which children were the most vocal? Were the girls as engaged as the boys? What were the forces influencing and shaping the individual students' contributions? – but the story was developing rapidly and a tangible sense of excitement and engagement in the group focused the mind on the activity in hand.

By the end of the session our short story was complete and there was obvious pride as we read together from the large sheets already hung around the class. The decision to make a class book of the story was quickly taken as the students were already very proud of what they had created and keen to share it with others. A follow-up session allowed us to discuss the book-making in more detail. In discussing a wide range of existing books, Meta and I explained some of the possibilities open to us. The students made group decisions about format, font and layout. Some of these decisions were made by voting, others by consensus. Again, I now wonder about the decision-making – was it as participatory as I like to think? Were *all* the students engaged? However differentiated individual inclusion and commitment might have been at the time, though, subsequent work with the class convinces me that most of the students developed a special relationship with the story. For some students, quieter involvement in such a decision-making process may have been an important learning experience, developing awareness and building confidence for future situations. Other more confident and experienced students were able to show leadership in the process, taking obvious pride at how the class as a whole acted upon their suggestions.

Jessica and Jordan meet an alien was then typed up in the chosen font, with each sentence or small section on a different page. Having worked out as a group what the different characters would look like, in order to maintain coherency through the book, the students worked in pairs to illustrate the pages. Much to the excitement of the authors, these pages were then spirally bound and enclosed in a plastic cover. A first reading of the finished product was an exciting, loud and very self-congratulatory choral reading! The story became a firm favourite with the students and certainly contributed to the development of a special sense of class community. It was kept on display in class and any visitor to the room was immediately assailed with it. *Jessica and Jordan* had certainly outlived and outgrown any of the expectations that Meta and I had at the start of the project.

Jessica and Jordan meet an alien: the bilingual editions

As part of the 'Storying in many tongues' project, five students from our local secondary school spent a day in school reading stories with different classes in their different first languages. Two of these Grade 9 students had prepared special stories in both English and in Tamil, made pictures and other props and had practised reading aloud for a young audience. Their visit was a great success, and especially so in Room 17 where their stories fell on attentive ears. The storytelling became a reciprocal activity, though, as the older students were not allowed to leave before listening to *Jessica and Jordan meet an alien.* Engaging successfully with the younger children, the older students then proceeded to interpret the story into their first languages, much to the delight of the second graders who for the first time were hearing their own story in their own languages. The class was already familiar with commercially produced bilingual texts, and very soon the suggestion was made to create our own bilingual versions of *Jessica and Jordan,* with written translations of their text. This suggestion was immediately seized upon, and children spoke of wanting to read it with their parents and other family members who spoke little English. Here was a way for them to connect their family with their school work – school work that they were obviously so proud of.

So began a time of seeking out potential translators, drawing on willing and able parents, community members known to the school, friends and family of the staff. It took some time for the 'volunteer' translators to return the completed texts. I was certainly aware of the impatience of the students, each eagerly asking when the edition in *their* language would be ready. At the same time, I was also aware of the time constraints of the adults involved and of the possible anxiety caused by a request for written, school-type work. The texts returned, often beautifully handwritten, providing us with the means to create our own dual text books. The completed different language versions still had to be combined with the English text and assembled into book form (a process which involved much cutting, pasting and copying). Having read Viv Edwards' *The Power of Babel* (1998), I was very conscious of issues around the relative positioning of the different languages' texts in the finished book. What does it say about the status of the language, for example, if the English appears twice as large as the Gujurati? What message is conveyed to the reader if the English is neatly word-processed and the Urdu handwritten? I tried to create a balance in the size of the texts and, where possible, to create equality for the language status in the books. For example, it was possible to word-process the Twi version of the story as Twi (spoken by Ghanaian students in the class) is written with the Latin alphabet, with the addition of a couple of extra characters which I was able to create on the computer. Word-processing was also possible for the Gujurati, Hindi and Punjabi versions, but resources were not available at the time to do the same for Tamil and Greek. Handwritten versions were the only way to respond to the students who were anxiously awaiting *Jessica and Jordan* in these languages.

The completion of each new edition of *Jessica and Jordan* created another occasion for community celebration in Room 17. I tried to arrange for a speaker of the second language to come to read aloud; each time was accompanied by the intense involvement of the students for whom this language was *theirs*. Their pride and pleasure was tangible; they were mouthing the words and chorusing some of the sections. Other students were also captivated by sounds and rhythms of the unfamiliar language, intrigued and impressed by otherwise hidden linguistic skills of their classmates. A spontaneous trilingual reading happened one day when a substitute teacher of Indian origin worked with the class. Her offer to read in Punjabi, Urdu and English was greeted with an enthusiastic 'Yeah!' from the Punjabi and the Urdu speakers. Unfortunately there were long faces from the Tamil speakers when she had to tell them that she didn't speak their language too. Despite initial disappointment, though, the whole class soon settled down to listen, fascinated by the different ways in which their story of Jessica and Jordan could now be expressed. One Tamil-speaker reprimanded another for his interruptions during an Urdu section: 'I just want to hear the story'.

The dual text books go home

Such was the enthusiasm for taking each new book home that arguments often had to be smoothed out and rotas established between the students. On a number of occasions I watched students clutching the book (by this stage a second or third generation photocopy, lacking the bright colours of the original) running to show parents and other family members meeting them from school. Although there was much support in the school and in the community for the 'Storying in many tongues' project, we were aware that some parents did feel concerned that their children should concentrate on learning English in school. I was keen to learn of parental responses to the bilingual *Jessica and*

Jordan books. I chatted informally to the students on the day after they had taken the story home and, although I do wonder to what extent the students told me what they imagined I would want to hear, their comments seemed to indicate that the book they had taken home so proudly had been well-received. It had given them a special opportunity to share a book with their parents and to show off to non-English speaking parents the extent of their fluency in English. The following quotes are just a few of the comments the children made:

> 'I like it so much. First I'll read it in English and then in my language,' said one girl. Her older sister confirmed that they did share the story at home. Mum and Grandma read *Jessica and Jordan* in Urdu and the younger daughter had impressed them with her English reading.

> 'I read it with my Mum,' described another. 'She read the Tamil.'
> 'And does she speak English?' I asked.
> 'No, she speaks Tamil.'
> 'So did you read the English?'
> 'Yes, she said I was good at speaking English. She said the pictures were good too.'

> 'My Dad read it in Urdu. When he finished he said to me to read it in English. When it was finished he said it was good. 'You read English so fast,' he said.

In talking about the project with students we stressed how important it is to make connections between the different languages that a person speaks, that by talking, reading and writing in one language, one develops skills important for any language. We hoped that this belief would be conveyed both explicitly and implicitly to the parents. There were certainly positive responses from home. Many parents became involved, translating the texts, storytelling in class, and others reading at home with students.

Beyond the storytelling

Bilingual editions of *Jessica and Jordan meet an alien* also provided opportunities for children to reflect on the written and spoken forms of their two languages and to engage in conversation about them in school. There is now a large body of research which confirms that this sort of meta-linguistic talk and awareness is of great importance for bilingual students to be able to successfully learn in their two languages and to shift their learning between the two (Edwards 1998). It supports the general cognitive development of bilingual learners, and enables them to vocalise their own individual ways of making sense of the world through two languages. 'My Dad will read it in Urdu. Urdu is hard because it is written the other way,' said Jeevan. (He demonstrates writing from right to left.) 'Sometimes I get confused and write Urdu like English' (laughing).

A simple story offers so many interesting aspects for study and further investigation. By focusing on the spoken language associated with it, I hope to draw attention to the way in which such a story, beginning with the process of its creation, has served to develop student oracy in multiple ways. Although closely linked to reading and writing, the creation of the story of *Jessica and Jordan* took place in an oral mode. Subsequent tellings of the story, and converstaions about the story in many different languages have, I believe, contributed to powerful feelings of ownership, involvement and 'authenticity' in the relationships the authors have developed with the written text of their story. *Jessica and Jordan* certainly live on; although part two may never actually be written, many different sequels surely exist in the minds of the students of Room 17 which may have been expressed and debated with friends and family in a number of different languages.

Jessica and Jordan meet an alien

Once upon a time, Jessica and Jordan went to the store.
They wanted to buy candy because they were hungry.
Jordan likes Smarties and Jessica likes chocolate.
But the shopkeeper was an alien from outer space!
The shopkeeper reached into a big jar full of worms and spiders and gave them to
    Jessica and Jordan.
They were disappointed and shocked.
They ran home as fast as they could and shut the door behind them.
They tried to tell the story to their Mother.
Their Mother didn't believe them so they told their Father.
They tried to persuade their Mom to go back to the store.
But she could not see the worms and the spiders.
They went outside and saw a spaceship.
They got scared and ran away …
… but they saw the alien get in and take off.

End of part one of the story.

Acknowledgement

In describing the storying and the exciting talk 'in many tongues', I wish to acknowledge the importance of the wonderful work of Room 17's class teacher, Meta Daras, and the enthusiastic leadership, involvement and support of the school principal, Elizabeth Glucksman. Without them, none of this work would have been possible.

References

Edwards, V. (1998) *The Power of Babel: Teaching and Learning in Multilingual Classrooms.* Stoke-on-Trent: Trentham Books.

Part 4

Talking about language

Chapter 16

Interthinking – The power of productive talk

Lyn Dawes

If we adults want children to understand us, each other, and the world better, we must provide them with the best tools for communication that we have at our disposal. The aim of this chapter is to examine the link between children's development as independent learners and their speaking and listening, or oracy, skills. Literacy is the most fundamental concern of the primary teacher, and its links with oracy are examined. I look at concepts of literacies which have arisen in response to new technology. By summarising some key points from research on literacy, oracy and learning, I then highlight a crucial aspect of spoken language: the ability to engage in *interthinking*. I go on to describe a classroom project designed to enhance children's oracy skills through direct teaching and the support of their peers. By this means, it seems possible to provide children with the speaking and listening skills they require in order to make the most of their learning experiences across the curriculum.

New literacies

The talk-focused classroom project described in this chapter has, like the National Curriculum for 2000 (DfEE 1999), an integral Information and Communications Technology (ICT) component. It is therefore necessary to look at some new definitions of literacy which have arisen as a response to new technology in classrooms. Helping children to become literate is a fundamental aim of primary classrooms. But 'literacy' keeps changing its definition to suit the changing times. What do we now think of as the skills of literacy, and how can we help children to acquire them? *The Concise Oxford Dictionary of Current English* (Fowler and Fowler 1964) defines literacy as: '*n.* ability to read and write'. So, literacy can be simply stated as the competence necessary to read and write. But reading and writing change over time. We have moved a long way from quill pens to roller-balls, with both the development of the printing press and the personal computer fundamentally altering the nature of people's engagement with text

(Spender 1995). The tools of literacy vary between cultures as well as across time. Children in school now are required to gain *electronic literacy*, that is, to become knowledgeable users of electronic media to create and interpret texts (Warschauer 1999, p. 11). The expressions 'computer literacy', 'network literacy' and 'online literacy' focus on new technology as a means of reading and writing. Understanding how to create and use hyperlinked, randomly organised electronic texts demands special skills. But it is important to remember that new technology is the medium for literate activity rather than a sort of literacy in itself. It is possible to use the Internet for creative construction of knowledge, or to provide distraction upon distraction (in the same way that it is possible to use books to read, or to decorate coffee tables). What we wish to teach children in school is not a minimum capacity to decode language, but communicative competence: the ability to judge and interpret texts, to articulate, clarify and restate how to identify and find answers to problems, to negotiate meaning, and communicate concepts (Warschauer 1999, p. 11). To achieve all this, we must put to use the medium of talk.

The way computers enable communication seems to have captivated many people. Visionary statements forecast the advent of the global village, in which people link with each other via electronic networks. In the UK, burgeoning home ownership of computers linked to the Internet has been mirrored by government initiatives to ensure that this new capacity is available in classrooms. The National Grid for Learning (NGfL) was set up to equip schools with the necessary hardware and connections to use computers for communication and to ensure that educationally relevant material became available to teachers and children (DfEE 1997). For teachers, there is great value in enlisting the support of technology to help children learn to communicate. Much attention has been given to the way rapid, interactive communication is now possible between people all over the planet; ICT has the potential to allow children to 'meet' and talk with others from anywhere, about anything. If such global interaction is to be of educational benefit, teachers must ensure that children are able to talk constructively to those around them, as well as to the physically disembodied contacts throughout the world. The project described in this chapter enabled children to engage in educationally effective discussion face-to-face, a necessary precursor to communicating online.

Oracy and interthinking in class

We can define oracy as competence with spoken language. Oracy underpins a child's competence to engage with the curriculum in schools, for example, through listening, questioning and answering, storytelling and the use of word play (Grugeon *et al.* 1998). These are highly valuable skills, which merit the attention of the class teacher. However, I am now going to concentrate on one distinctive aspect of oracy – that of learners using talk to think together. This important function of talk is also known as interthinking. Interthinking is the 'joint, coordinated intellectual activity which people regularly accomplish using language' (Mercer 2000, p. 16).

Interthinking means thinking collectively. It involves people combining their mental resources to enable them to solve problems, or to plan and carry out actions together. The most useful medium for interthinking is talk, because talk allows rapid reflection and response. Speaking and listening is the child's primary access to the minds of other people. The ability to engage in interthinking may be of crucial importance to the child's development as an independent learner. Children's competence in speaking and listening will contribute immeasurably to their growing personal competence across the curriculum.

In order to explain the process of interthinking more fully, I will first provide background information about some theories of learning from which the concept arose. The following brief notes are not intended to summarise the complex works which they draw on, but to offer ways into considering some ideas which are of practical importance to teachers. The aspects of learning I will look at here are:

* Learning as a social activity
* Learning as community joining
* Learning in practice – scaffolding in the classroom.

Learning as a social activity

The Russian psychologist Lev Vygotsky described language as a tool for thinking, with the child's spoken language their earliest and most direct way to make meaning from their experiences. Talk is a social activity which enables the child to make meaning of what happens. Spoken language, developed and consolidated through interaction with others, shapes the ways people think. It affects both the way they think together when talking, and the way individuals think alone (Vygotsky 1978, Bruner 1978). Language structures, vocabulary and grammar – 'ways with words' (Brice Heath 1983) – heard during conversations or stories, induct children into the social world around them.

Learning as community joining

Jean Lave and Etienne Wenger (1991) studied learning taking place within individuals who are involved with others in a context, or a community of practice. We can consider a group of people who all know how to do a certain task as a community. (For example, the community may be members of an orchestra about to play Beethoven's Ninth symphony or a group of children about to carry out a science investigation.) The features of communities which are important here are that their members have the bonds of common knowledge and purpose: and that they understand one another when using the specialised vocabulary particular to the activity (e.g. 'a semi-quaver rest', 'a fair test').

Communities require new members for their stability and continuance. But how do new members gain all the skills and understanding they must have? Firstly, beginners are granted special 'newcomer' status. They are expected to tackle simplified tasks so that they can achieve success without their lack of expertise presenting risk to the community. A novice oboe player, for example, could expect to spend time practising with smaller groups or playing to audiences sympathetic to beginners before performing with a well-established orchestra. A child not proficient with science equipment might be grouped with others who are more experienced, and, for example, shown how to take temperatures with a thermometer before having to take readings crucial to the group's results. Learning takes place as the newcomer joins in with the specialised discourse of the community and progresses from being a peripheral member of the group towards becoming capable of achieving the community's purpose. Oracy is the most important tool for learning how to become a community member.

Learning in practice – scaffolding in the classroom

Jerome Bruner introduced the idea of scaffolding to describe how learning is a joint achievement (Bruner 1978, Mercer 1995). During the process of teaching and learning, Bruner describes how teachers 'lend' their mental capacities to learners in order to support and shape the learning. The term 'scaffolding' uses the metaphor of a structure that provides essential support, but which can be removed once a construction can stand alone. In school, understanding is constructed within the supporting framework of the talk between teachers and learners.

Children can be moved through a difficult task in simple stages by a supportive 'teacher' – who may be adult or a peer. Support is gradually reduced as the learner makes the jump from not knowing to knowing at each stage. Here it is useful to bring in Vygotsky's idea that learners exhibit a *zone of proximal development* (zpd) – that is, a person scaffolding learning can gauge what step the learner is ready for next: what they can achieve with support, and might then go on to achieve alone. The primary teacher, having a close working relationship with a group of children, is uniquely placed to assess the zpd of the individuals in her or his care. The teacher can provide the scaffolding through talk that enables children to develop competence, to move on – to learn. In the talk-focused classroom, the teacher can equip the learners with the awareness and skills that they require in order to work in groups together, and so effectively scaffold one another's learning.

The value of interthinking

Our ability to use spoken language to communicate our thinking with one another is one of our greatest human assets. Interthinking describes the situation that exists when two or more people achieve real communication with each other, when mental resources are pooled through the medium of talk. In this way people can achieve more together than they ever could have achieved separately. Since this is one of the most effective means of learning, we need to teach pupils how to become competent at interthinking.

During my research study into teachers' use of computers in classrooms, I asked groups of primary teachers to describe the sort of talk that they hoped would go on between children working together in groups. The answers always included the ideas that children should:

- listen to each other;
- respect the thoughts and ideas of others in the group;
- compromise if there is disagreement;
- give reasons to support opinions, arguments or ideas;
- give everyone the opportunity to participate;
- respond to what other people say;
- share and explain ideas.

What teachers were hoping would happen during group work was that children would engage with each others' minds through talking together. They wanted interthinking. Grouping children around computers provided a context for the articulation of thoughts. Socio-cultural theories of learning (like those summarised above) indicate that by putting their thoughts into words, learners understand their own ideas, and those of others, more clearly. Children talking together gain new insights from one another and develop new knowledge through joint explorations of ideas. In some classes, however, there may be too few children who have experienced this kind of discussion to be able to act as 'discourse guides' for others. Many children are uncertain how to take on this role, or have no confidence in themselves, or the other members of their group, to lead discussions. Group work is disrupted and learning falls away, if children who do not know how to talk constructively to one another revert to socialising, demanding, asserting, ordering, disrupting – or to silence. It is unwise to assume that children know how to talk productively to one another (Wegerif and Scrimshaw 1997). The next section of this chapter provides a summary of a project on oracy skills which was successful in helping children to learn how to talk effectively to each other when working in groups.

Raising Achievement Through Thinking with Language Skills (RATTLS)

The RATTLS project, which took place in a group of primary schools in the late 1990s, built on two previous projects: Spoken Language and New Technology (SLANT) and Talk, Reasoning and Computers (TRAC). References to the outcomes of these projects are at the end of the chapter. I will summarise key points, and try to provide enough information for teachers either to develop their own projects, or to access the material produced for teachers as a result of the research.

The RATTLS project involved classes of Year 5 children in the feeder primary schools of a large secondary school in Milton Keynes. The classes which had enrolled in the project were taught a series of specially designed talk lessons by their teachers. Matched classes in the city acted as controls. Assessment took place by considering the children's talk together, and by asking the children to complete non-verbal reasoning tests before and after the intervention. (For more information about the talk lessons and research see Dawes, Wegerif and Mercer, 2000.)

Key issues emerging from the action research were:

(a) The need to clarify ground rules for talk.
(b) Teaching talking lessons.
(c) Exploratory talk and children's own ground rules.
(d) The role of ICT in supporting talk.
(e) Using talk to learn across the curriculum.
(f) Outcomes of the 'Talking Lessons' approach.

(a) Ground rules for talk

The Open University research team observing children working in groups at computers were dismayed to find very little evidence of educationally effective talk. But teachers like myself were even more dismayed. The researchers compiled a list of 'Ground rules for effective talk', rules which if adhered to by groups could enable productive work together. You might like to compare the following list with the teachers' list given in the previous section (p. 128).

Ground rules for effective talk in groups:

- all relevant information is shared;
- the group takes responsibility for decisions;
- reasons are expected;
- challenges are accepted;
- alternatives are discussed before a decision is taken;
- all in the group are encouraged to speak by other group members;
- the group seeks to reach agreement.

(b) Teaching the talking lessons

A series of ten one-hour lessons were devised which incorporated an explanation of the ground rules and provided activities for practice. Each lesson was designed to increase the children's awareness of themselves as people who use talk to get things done. Children worked in mixed ability groups of three. The lessons had three parts:

(i)   The aims of the lesson, to do with the quality and purpose of the talk, were made explicit to the children.
(ii) A group activity, which was clarified by the teacher before groups began work by talking to one another around a given context.
(iii) A whole-class discussion, in which the class decided whether they had achieved the stated aims and presented feedback from their group.

(c) Exploratory talk and children's own ground rules

Video evidence of children who had taken the talk training showed that they had gained an understanding of what was meant by, 'Talk together to decide …'. Effective talk between learners, what Douglas Barnes called *exploratory talk* (Barnes and Todd 1977), can be summarised as follows:

1. Children engage critically but constructively with each others' ideas.
2. Statements and suggestions are offered for joint consideration. These may be challenged and counter-challenged, but challenges are justified by explicit reasons, and alternative hypotheses are offered.
3. Knowledge is made publicly accountable, and reasoning is evident in the talk.
4. Progress is made towards eventual joint agreement.

(Adapted from Mercer 1995)

With some experience of the talking lessons, classes were asked to suggest and agree on their own personalised set of ground rules for talk. These ground rules provided the structure that groups needed in their efforts to discuss issues and support one another's learning through talk. A class set of ground rules follows. It is interesting to compare it with the research ground rules, and the teachers' ideas.

Class 5D's ground rules for talk:

1. Discuss things, ask for opinions, ask for reasons why, listen to people.
2. Think before you speak.
3. Respect other people's ideas, don't just use your own.
4. Concentrate.
5. Make sure that the group agrees after talking.

It seemed that it was possible for everyone to agree and to say quite simply what sort of talk should be going on. The necessary step was to focus the children on their own growing talk proficiency. As you can see, rule 2 and rule 4 are slightly unusual, but the children felt they were important. There is no overt mention of including all group members, but rule 5 implies that this has been accepted.

(d) ICT supporting talk

Specially written software supported the children's attempts to engage one another in exploratory talk (Wegerif and Dawes 1998). The software provided open-ended problems for discussion, with screen prompts which said, 'Talk together and decide what to do'. Children who had not undertaken talk training ignored this prompt and carried on rapidly to the next screen. But talk-focused children sat back and very deliberately solicited one another's views, discussing issues until they decided how they could agree. As a result their work at the computer was much more productive.

(e) Using talk to learn across the curriculum

The skills required to think collaboratively can be taught, but require much practice. The entire curriculum provides opportunities for such work. Science and maths investigations, art projects, a consideration of historical artefacts, drama and team work in physical education, citizenship issues and literacy, all benefit from talk. Pointing out to learners the aims for their talk together before they begin work is an important strategy which enhances learning.

(f) Outcomes of the 'Talking lessons' approach

The research indicated that groups of children who had received talk training did better in non-verbal reasoning tests than those who had not had training. We concluded from this that the talk-focused children had learnt how to engage more effectively with one another's ideas. We also used a test of non-verbal reasoning skills as a way of assessing the children's reasoning ability before and after the talk training. The test revealed individual development in reasoning ability: children who had learnt to reason collaboratively could now reason better when working alone. We deduced that they had internalised the way of thinking that is exploratory talk, with its capacity to use reasoning to solve problems. This development had been achieved completely through the medium of speaking and listening, as Vygotsky's learning theory had predicted. Our intention of 'raising achievement' in thinking through oracy had proved achievable. Naturally, such gain was not consistent throughout the children in our study, children exhibit mixed abilities in oracy as in any other area of learning, and some would need a little longer to gain competence. Also, our study indicated that those achieving least at the beginning of the intervention had made the largest gains by the end. Children whose out-of-school experiences had not included everyday access to reasoned discussion had few resources to draw on when required to work in a group. Such children benefited greatly from the talk training.

Conclusion

Spoken language is a fundamental tool for thought. Providing children with direct guidance, tuition and overt models of reasoning through talk can help them to acquire the speaking and listening skills which characterise successful independent learners. Talking lessons described in this chapter have been found to be successful in developing such skills.

ICT can be enlisted to support teachers in this task, by providing motivating, interactive contexts for discussion. ICT also provides a rapid, wide-ranging medium about which communication can take place. The capacity of new technology to aid communication may be its best application in education, but computers do not teach children *how* to think. Their function is to provide a context for practice. The teacher's role in harnessing the technology to the aims of the talk-focused classroom is therefore crucial. 'If online literacy is to rise above the level of the bells and whistles of high-powered Nintendo games, it must be in support of the same collective task of human transformation that has characterised our experience of print literacy' (Tubman 1992).

A classroom community is the unique construction of its component teacher(s) and learners, and in this lies its strength. The ability of learning communities to pool experience, ideas and intentions, and to come to joint solutions through talk is a powerful means to get things done. It also enables success for the many rather than isolated attainment for the few. By providing children with oracy skills that enable them to support one another through constructive conversations, the teacher equips children with the tools to learn more effectively. Children proficient in talk can expect to put this capacity to good use across the curriculum, and in any area of life where good communication helps solve problems.

References

Barnes, D. and Todd, F. (1977) *Communication and Learning in Small Groups*. London: Routledge and Kegan Paul.

Brice Heath, S. (1983) *Ways with Words: Language, Life and Work in Communities and Classrooms*. Cambridge: Cambridge University Press.

Bruner, J. S. (1978) 'The role of dialogue in language acquisition', in Sinclair, A., Jarvella, R. and Levelt, W. (eds) *The Child's Conception of Language*. New York: Springer-Verlag.

Dawes, L., Wegerif, R. and Mercer, N. (2000, in press) *Talking and Thinking: A pack for Key Stage 2 teachers and learners*. London: Questions Publishing.

DfEE (1997) *Connecting the learning society*. London: HMSO.

DfEE/QCA (1999) The National Curriculum: Handbook for primary teachers in England and Wales. London: DfEE/QCA.

Fowler, H. W. and Fowler, F. G.(eds) (1964) *The Concise Oxford Dictionary of Current English* 5th edn. Oxford: Oxford University Press.

Grugeon, E., *et al.* (1998) *Teaching Speaking and Listening in the Primary School*. London: David Fulton Publishers.

Lave, J. and Wenger, E. (1991) *Situated Learning: Legitimate Peripheral Participation*. Cambridge: Cambridge University Press.

Mercer, N. (1995) *The Guided Construction of Knowledge: Talk amongst Teachers and Learners*. Clevedon: Multilingual Matters.

Mercer, N. (2000) *Words and minds*. London: Routledge.

Spender, D. (1995) *Nattering on the Net: Women, Power and Cyberspace*. Melbourne: Spinifex Press.

Tubman, M. (1992) *Word perfect: Literacy in the Computer Age*. Pittsburg, PA: University of Pittsburg Press.

Vygotsky, L. (1978) *Mind in society*. Cambridge, Mass.: Harvard University Press.

Warschauer, M. (1999) 'Electronic literacies: language, culture and power,' in *Online Education*. Mahwah, NJ: Erlbaum Associates.

Wegerif, R. and Dawes, L. (1998) 'Encouraging exploratory talk around computers', in Monteith, M. (ed.) *IT for Learning Enhancement*. Exeter: Intellect Books.

Wegerif, R. and Scrimshaw, P. (1997) *Computers and Talk in the Primary Classroom*. Clevedon: Multilingual Matters.

Chapter 17

Checking on the checker –
Using computers to talk about spelling and grammar

Michael Lockwood

Chaucer at his laptop/auto-checking his screenplay proposal for spelling and style.
(Simon Armitage, *Killing Time*, Faber 1999)

Word 97, the word-processing software I am using to type this, incorporates a spelling and grammar checker, Spell It, which operates as you type. As users will know, the checker underlines words it cannot find in its dictionary with a red wavy line, and possible grammatical errors with a green one. For example, as I was writing this, the checker suggested I put a hyphen in 'word processing' when I used it as an adjective in my first sentence (though not when used as a noun as in this sentence). However, the checker also underlined 'first' in green and suggested changing it to 'firsts', assuming a structure that needs a plural, a suggestion I chose to ignore. This nicely illustrates the pros and cons of this software. Users tend to be alternately infuriated and intrigued by the suggestions the checker makes. Some writers, of course, (and maybe you are one), take up the option of switching the automatic checker off, and simply running a spell-check at the end in the conventional way. They are often annoyed by the grammatical suggestions the checker routinely makes: for example, suggesting 'that' for 'which' to introduce a relative clause, and underlining use of the passive voice. However, Spell It needs to be differentiated very carefully from AutoCorrect, another feature of *Word 97*. AutoCorrect will silently correct common spelling and grammar errors as you type (for example, missing capital letters). There is no underlining or dialogue box to respond to, and as a writer it is easy to become reliant on the AutoCorrect facility.

Whatever our personal preferences as writers, as teachers Spell It offers a valuable tool to make children more aware of spelling and grammar choices when they write or edit their work. As *Word 97* becomes increasingly available in the primary school, teachers will inevitably be faced with the question of how to make use of its automatic spell-checker. Undoubtedly there will be times when teachers will want to switch it off, and allow young writers to concentrate on composition or to demonstrate their secretarial skills unaided. What I would like to suggest in this chapter is that there should also be times when teachers exploit the interactive nature of Spell It to develop children's knowledge about spelling and grammar *through dialogue*, both with the computer, with the teacher and with each other.

Research background

Previous research has shown the value of collaborative talk for learning in the primary classroom, including the type of exploratory talk I want to focus on in this chapter (Barnes and Todd 1977, 1995). The advent of new technology has made it even more important to retain this dialogue with others in the learning situation, avoiding the danger that the computer used for writing is seen as a replacement for the teacher or other pupils. As Buckingham and Sefton-Green (1993) stress: 'The critical need is to ensure that production remains a collaborative, social process ... [one of] dialogue between the student, the screen, the teacher and other students.' One beneficial effect of the shortage of computers in primary classrooms over the past twenty years has been that collaborative working by children has been a necessity, just to ensure that everyone got a turn. Now with the increasing advent of computer suites in primary schools, the possibilities of purely individual work are increasing. It is probably a good time, therefore, to remind ourselves of the sound educational as well as logistical reasons for children working in pairs or small groups with a computer. As Kuhn and Stannard (1997) point out: 'children do tend to talk to each other more when they are working with a computer. This can sometimes be dismissed as chat, but usually involves at least an element of exploration and discovery.' As long ago as 1990, Anthony Adams expressed the need for more research in this area: 'We urgently need more studies of the ways in which the uses of the new technology can be applied for the enhancement and development of group processes in speaking and listening activities.' Mercer *et al.* (1991) set up the Open University Spoken Language and New Technologies (SLANT) project to look at just this area, reporting that

> one of the potential virtues of the computer as an educational resource is its capacity for a dynamic presentation of information and interest in a way that is often difficult to achieve in other kinds of collaborative activity. Moreover, the screen presentation facilitates a sharing of information and provides a source of contextual reference for shared knowledge and activity in a way that written texts cannot.

It has always been recognised that computer spell-checkers have benefits for the presentation of children's work, particularly for children with literacy learning difficulties or those for whom presentation is a particular problem (Brown and Howlett 1994). However, commentators have also pointed to the further possibilities which electronically stored text offers: 'there is considerable potential here for knowledge about language activities which would not have been accessible to students previously' (Abbott 1993).

The Kingman Report of 1988 (DES 1988), an inquiry into the teaching of English language in schools, foreshadowed this approach in its advice:

> The word processor, with its ability to shape, delete and move text around, provides the means by which pupils can achieve a satisfactory product. Through the use of word processors pupils are drawn into explicit discussion of the nature and likely impact of what they write. They will begin to talk about appropriate structures, correct punctuation and spelling and the vocabulary appropriate for their audience.

In this chapter I want to suggest how the use of the most sophisticated software such as *Word 97* can become a teaching aid to develop literacy skills, knowledge about language and oracy.

The project

In what follows I will draw upon some small-scale research I carried out in a local West Berkshire school which has *Word 97* as part of the *RM Window Box* used in its recently equipped, open-plan computer suite. The activities described were carried out with a group of Year 6 pupils during a number of visits I made to the school in the second half of the summer term 2000.

First session

The six children of mixed ability I worked with were familiar with the use of a spell-checker, but said that they would usually do a spell-check at the end of their work by clicking on the toolbar icon rather than by using the right-hand mouse button as they typed. After an initial demonstration and discussion of the Spell It tool, I gave the children the sheet shown in Figure 17.1, adapted from previous research into children's awareness of standard English (Lockwood, 1999). The aim of the activity was to assess the use of the spell-checker for developing awareness of standard and non-standard forms in writing through collaborative, exploratory talk. The children worked in pairs at the computers, and, with their agreement, I tape-recorded their conversations.

Checking on the checker

Type in the sentences below <u>exactly as on the sheet</u>. Remember to put in the full-stops at the end. The computer will underline some words with a red or green wavy line. Click on the <u>right-hand</u> button on the mouse to find out why the words are underlined. The computer will usually give you some suggestions for how you could change them, or you can choose to **Ignore All** the suggestions. Talk to your partner about why the words are underlined and whether you think you should change them. <u>Are there any other words that you think need changing?</u> Can you work out what the difference is between red and green underlining?

1. **Type your names first and see what happens.**
2. **He doesn't know nothing hisself.**
3. **We ain't got none.**
4. **We done our work proper.**
5. **I fell off of the wall.**
6. **That's the boy what I told you about.**
7. **I never seen nobody.**
8. **She was the beautifulest of the two women.**
9. **They wasn't late.**
10. **I could of told you the answer.**
11. **He's gotten into trouble.**
12. **Me and my dad paid five pound to go up London.**
13. **There was alot of mistakes in my letter.**
14. **I dunno what's wrong with that.**
15. **Tests is boring!**

Figure 17.1

The computer's response to the children's surnames provoked much discussion. I had initially demonstrated how the checker suggested I change my name to *Locoweed*, but some of the children's surnames were dictionary words and therefore not underlined, provoking the comment: 'It hasn't underlined it! That's not fair!' and discussion about why this had happened. Where names were underlined in red, much amusement was had ('Do the suggestions again!'). As the children moved on to typing in the sentences in non-standard English, productive discussion began to be generated. Spell It underlined some of the non-standard forms in green (*ain't, wasn't, could of, me and my dad, there, tests is*) and some in red (*hisself, beautifulest, alot, dunno*), but the suggested corrections were not reliable for *alot, dunno* and *me and my dad*, and no suggestion was offered for *beautifulest*. The three pairs varied in their responses to the activity.

Chris and Jamie noticed that the computer immediately underlined *hisself* in red in the first sentence, but did not underline *nothing* in green until *hisself* was corrected and the cursor moved onto a new line. After discussion they decided to adopt the strategy of not only putting in a full stop, as I had suggested, but of entering text in order to make the checker kick in. In other words, their exploratory talk was about the best procedures for operating the software, as well as about the language issues involved in the activity. As the pair went on through the sentences, Jamie spotted the errors not underlined by Spell It: *off of* ('It hasn't changed!'), *proper*, and *what I*. Because they were rather slow at typing, Jamie and Chris completed about half of the sentences in the 20 minutes or so available. As a pairing, though, the two boys, one of above average ability and one below, successfully interacted and shared the activity.

Amy and Antony, another pairing of above and below average abilities, interacted rather less in their boy/girl pairing than Jamie and Chris. They worked more quickly and completed most of the sentences, but at the end had accepted non-standard features which the computer had not underlined, such as *proper, what I, they wasn't, gotten* and *five pound*. Antony was aware that some of these sounded wrong, but was not able to convince his partner to overrule the computer. Careful thought clearly needs to go into the pairings used for activities such as this to ensure a working partnership. Although the computer underlined *beautifulest* in red, the pair noticed that it gave no suggestions when the right-hand button was clicked. Amy was unsure what to do, but Antony suggested *most beautiful*, whereupon the computer put a wavy green line under *most* and suggested *more*, and the pair accepted this after some discussion about which sounded right.

The third pairing of two average ability girls, Lucy and Emma, was a slightly unequal one in terms of involvement, with Lucy taking the lead most of the time. This pair also had problems with *beautifulest*. They decided to investigate this spelling further by changing the word to *ugliest*, which was immediately underlined and *uglier* suggested. The pair agreed on *uglier one* finally. There was then some discussion about whether *beautifuler one* was allowable before time ran out. At the end, they had accepted *off of* and *gotten*, both non-standard British forms not underlined by the spell-checker.

Second session

For the second session, I designed a task (Figure 17.2) that involved less typing in of text in order to allow a maximum focus on the checking and discussion aspects of the activity. The emphasis this time was on exploring spelling rather than non-standard grammar through dialogue with the spell-checker and a partner. The children worked in the same pairings at revising this text, which was already loaded into the computer for them.

45 Megabyte Towers
Window Box
PC1 1RM

Dear Childern,

I understand ewe are interested in what computers now about spelling and grammer, so I'm righting to explain what I do. my job is to check all the langauge that goes through this computor. A big job I think youll agree. I 'm the first to admit that I'm not prefect at it and I sometimes miss things which should be corrected. also I sometimes underline things in red or green which are not mistakes Well so would you if the words weren't in your dictionry. I think you'll agree tho that I do a useful job, if you use me properly, and I can teach you things about langauge as well as make your righting sound better. well must get back to work now. While I've been away no one's been checking the words going through the computer so goodness nows what's been coming out. Better check it yourselfs this time!

Regards from,

S.P.L. Checker

Figure 17.2

I asked the children to use Spell It to check the underlined words and discuss suggested changes. I also asked them to check for other errors not picked out by the computer. From the tape recordings of the children's talk, it was clear there was more interaction this time, as the partners were more familiar with each other and the task set. There was a lot of evidence on the tape of the children thinking aloud, particularly the girls: the presence of a trusted partner seemed to facilitate a sharing of 'inner language' and thought processes. The boy/girl pairing of Amy and Antony, in particular, operated better this time as they jointly made decisions on spelling, for example:

Antony:	(reading) 'I am writing'
Amy:	Aren't there two 't's in writing?
Antony:	It doesn't think so.
Amy:	Oh well.

Antony became interested in why the computer underlined sentences that appeared to be correct (*Also I sometimes underline things in red or green which are not mistakes*): 'If I take out the full stop it says it's right, and if I put the full stop back it underlines *Also I sometimes underline* and says it's a fragment, but it's got no suggestions!' Whereas Antony found this an intriguing puzzle, his partner Amy, a self-confessed technophobe ('I hate the things!') found it frustrating: 'Silly computer! We're not getting anywhere are we?' However, Amy did find it amusing to go through the suggestions for some of the underlined spelling errors, when Antony tactfully prompted her:

Amy:	(typing) 'I dunno'. I don't? (number 14 from the first sheet, which they were finishing off)
Antony:	Shall we see what it says?

Amy: (goes through all suggestions in funny voice) I dun, I dune, I Duane, I duenna, I dung! God, ignore all suggestions! (Amy speaks to me) It underlined this, 'dunno.'

Antony: It didn't say anything helpful though.

As far as the checking the letter was concerned the children had for the most part corrected the spelling and grammar mistakes underlined, but had failed to notice other mistakes not underlined, such as *now, righting* and *prefect.* This suggested that the visible evidence of a spell-check had put them off their guard, despite my instructions to scrutinise the text for other errors.

In a general discussion at the end, I asked the six children to reflect on the activity and on their use of word processing and spell-checkers both in and out of school. The group said they received no specific training in the use of *Word 97* (this was confirmed by their teacher) and that any pupils could use the program for their writing. (In the *RM Window Box* package in use in the school, the Yellow, Green and Blue options gave access to *Talking First Word*, and Red to *Word 97.*) The children's own practice with spell-checkers, they confirmed, was to check at the end of their work, or possibly half way through or at the end of a section. They were unanimous in agreeing that the spell-checker was useful, particularly when writing was being done for display or 'if you're rushing'. They did not feel the spell-checker made them lazy as writers because, as Chris pointed out: 'Sometimes the spell-checker gets it wrong. It misses things and it doesn't underline them.' Amy defended the spell-checker as a tool for learning: 'When you correct it on the computer, you learn the words and then if you have to do it again you can just type it in.' Four of the six children said they had computers at home with similar word-processing programs. Antony looked forward to the next generation of spell-checkers which he felt would be able to correct punctuation, which *Word 97* does not. Jamie hoped in the future the program would be able to give you 'descriptive words'.

Third session

For our third session I designed an activity which enabled the six children to work together with me in a 'guided writing' situation, as used in the literacy hour, to try to assess the potential for using Spell It in this context. I took the teaching objective for the lesson from the *NLS Framework* (DfEE 1998) for Year 6 Term 3 Sentence Level 3: 'to revise formal styles of writing: the impersonal voice, the use of passives …'. I felt that this was an objective which Spell It could certainly help with and one which was difficult to make interesting in more conventional ways. The children were grouped around a table in front of a single computer which I operated; the text in Figure 17.3 was displayed in a large font size.

The session was very successful in raising awareness of the use of passive sentences in formal writing and in generating productive group talk. I began by asking the group what they thought formal writing was ('not chatty, posh … say if you were writing to a bank manager or something'). I asked the group to guess how many words were in the passage. I then ran the spell-checker on the passage but ignored all the suggested changes in order to get to the Readability Statistics given at the end of the checker (these may need to be switched on by ticking the box in the Spelling and Grammar tab of the Options given under the Tools menu on the *Word 97* menu bar). We looked at the word count (171) and at the other information given, especially the percentage of passive sentences (80 per cent) and the US Grade Level given for the passage (6.9, which gives a reading age of 11.9).

Formal writing

It has been said by someone that spell checkers are a bad thing. It was claimed that spell checkers encourage children to be careless in their writing, because they know their mistakes will be spotted by the checker. Children have said to me, however, that they think spell checkers are useful. I think it all depends how these programs are used by children. If they are used to encourage children to think carefully about the words they are using, then that is a good thing. If they are used by children without thinking, then this could be a bad thing. Mistakes are made by spell checkers and the writer still has to be careful in looking for mistakes which have been missed by the computer. Perhaps in the future all our writing will be done for us by computers that can understand our voice. Perhaps hardly any mistakes will be missed by the computer of the future. At the moment, though, we still need to check up on the checker.

Figure 17.3

Some of the children had encountered the terms active and passive previously, but I recapped the features of passive sentences. I asked the group to help me make the writing less formal by changing the passive sentences to active ones using the spell-checker. We went through the passage looking at the seven clauses or sentences underlined in green by the checker, discussing possible changes first and then comparing the spell-checker's suggestions. The children quickly picked up the use of 'by' as a marker for passive constructions, and soon grew in confidence in their suggestions for how to change the passive voice to active. In some cases the group decided (by democratic vote!) to over-rule the checker's suggestions and rewrite a clause manually, as when the checker suggested *if children without thinking use them* rather than the group's preferred *if children use them without thinking*. The group endorsed my comment that it's good to have a human checker as well and that you mustn't switch off your own checker when working on the computer. A nice example of this came when the checker suggested *spell checkers makes mistakes* ('That's right that is!' agreed Jamie) and missed the passive construction later in the same sentence: *mistakes which have been missed by the computer.* As we went on with the activity, the children grew more adept at producing active versions of the underlined clauses. For example, Lucy confidently translated: *Perhaps in the future computers that can understand our voice will do all our writing for us.* This exchange about the following clause illustrates how the activity developed effective collaborative group talk for problem solving, as well as increasing skill in changing passives:

Chris:	'In the future, hardly any mistakes will be made by the computer'
ML:	Ah, but we've still got a 'by' haven't we ...
Chris:	Oh yeah.
Lucy:	'In the future, computers won't make any mistakes ...'
Jamie:	'Hardly any mistakes will be missed. ... The computer of the future will miss hardly any mistakes.'
Chris:	That sounds good. I like that one.

After we'd finished checking the passage, I read it through in the new version and we agreed it sounded less formal and was easier to read and understand. I asked the group to guess the number of words, the percentage of passive sentences and the reading level now, before revealing the Readability Statistics. They were intrigued to find that although the word count had only gone down a little (from 171 to156), the percentage of passive sentences had fallen dramatically (from 80 per cent to 20 per cent) and the Grade Level had been reduced from 6.9 to 6.6 (11.6 years). To finish the session, we tried changing the Writing Style of the spell-checker from Standard to Casual and then to Formal (choosing from the Spelling and Grammar tab of Options from the Tools menu). We discovered that a Casual spell-check underlined nothing in the passage, while a Formal spell-check underlined nine things in the passage, including *are used* (passive voice, no suggestions) and *At the moment* ('Now' suggested). The group were again intrigued by this and their interest in the session and participation in it were maintained until the end. Inevitably, there was more talk from me in this session, and a tendency for two of the boys, Jamie and Chris, unintentionally to dominate the discussion at times, yet overall I was pleased with the level of interaction, motivation and involvement of all the group of five (Amy was absent).

At the end of the session Lucy revealed another use she had found for the spell-checking facility we had been exploring: 'I used the spell-checker last night. With our homework we had to do anagrams ... so say it was 'heart' it was 'earth' right ... and so what I did was I wrote it up in my computer but muddled up and it gave me the answers 'cos I couldn't work some of them out so it gave you the answers.'

Conclusions

The small-scale project described here certainly confirmed for me previous research findings about the value of using computers to develop an articulate as well as literate classroom. For example, two of the findings of the SLANT project borne out by my own small-scale research were: '(i) that computers can be used effectively to support the teaching and learning of exploratory talk; and (ii) that computer supported collaborative learning can serve to integrate peer learning with directed teaching (Mercer *et al.* 1991).

Earlier research has also pointed out how computers aid motivation: 'The involvement on a joint task with the computer encourages focused discussion and argument, giving a reality to oral work, which it might have lacked at other times' (Collins 1993). This was undoubtedly the case with the pair and group activities I carried out. Even earlier, Mallett and Newsome (1977) stressed that the computer can encourage pupil collaboration because 'it can move the teacher away from the role of expert into the role of collaborator. In the "expert" role the teacher will tend to do most of the talking, his or her utterance being "an extended monologue", that of his [sic] pupils, short answers to his questions.' In the activities described here I quite deliberately took on the role of collaborator rather than expert, even during the guided group session. In this I was influenced throughout by a comment of Hope (1985): 'It is the interaction between the child, the teacher, the program and his/her peers that is important.'

As well as 'placing new demands on our definition of literacy' (Kuhn and Stannard 1997), ICT also provides new opportunities for developing all aspects of a twenty-first century literacy. The use of ICT not only enhances literacy skills, defined as including speaking and listening, but also raises awareness of language itself, its structure and variation. This is recognised in the new National Curriculum where the use of ICT across the curriculum is required: 'Pupils should be given opportunities to apply and develop their ICT capability through the use of ICT tools to support their learning in all subjects' (DfEE/QCA 2000, p. 39). In the programmes of study for ICT at Key Stage 2, specifically, there is a requirement for 'Reviewing, modifying and evaluating work as it progresses', and in order to achieve this 'pupils should be taught to: describe and *talk about* the effectiveness of their work with ICT, comparing it with other methods ...' (p. 101) (my italics). There are obvious opportunities for meeting this requirement in the kind of activities outlined in this chapter. These activities also help to meet more specific requirements in the National Curriculum for English, in particular the need for pupils 'to develop their writing on paper and on screen' and 'to check their spelling using word banks, dictionaries and spellcheckers' (p. 56). In addition to developing these aspects of the ICT and writing programmes, the activities carried out also develop skills of 'group discussion and interaction' mentioned in the Speaking and Listening programmes of study at Key Stage 2.

The use of ICT in the ways described in this chapter can also fit easily into the organisation of the literacy hour, as part of independent group or pair work, or as part of guided writing and reading sessions. These activities can be used as ways to achieve the teaching objectives set out in the *NLS Framework for Teaching* (DfEE 1998). As well as exploring standard English forms, spelling errors and the passive voice, as here, other sentence and word level objectives at Key Stage 2 which involve investigation into aspects of grammar and spelling could also be approached in this way. For example:

- explorations of spelling rules through giving pupils lists of misspelled words to correct with the help of the checker;
- investigations into constructing words using prefixes, roots and suffixes using the computer to check for dictionary words;
- language investigations of the kind suggested for Year 6, involving dialect or American English;
- investigations of synonyms and antonyms, using the computer's thesaurus.

In *An Evaluation of the First Year of the NLS* (1999), OFSTED reports that ICT was often used inappropriately or not at all in the literacy hour: 'In the autumn term the independent work element of many literacy hours included the use of ICT by a group of pupils; unfortunately the work on which they were involved was often unrelated to the objectives of the lesson and too frequently was little more than low-level drill practice. However, as teachers became more proficient and confident in the teaching of literacy, they recognised the shortcomings of the unplanned use of ICT during literacy hours. By the summer term, this had the consequence of teachers making much less use of ICT during literacy hours.' More positive uses of ICT are also described: 'On the occasions when ICT was well used, pupils knew how to use tools such as the spell checker or thesaurus, and could edit confidently a text already loaded on the computer' (p. 19).

Having just had my writing underlined in green for 'Wordiness' (no suggestions), this is probably a fitting point at which to end!

References

Abbott, C. (1993) 'Information technology and English: looking ahead', *The English and Media Magazine*, Summer, no. 28.

Adams, A. (1990) 'The potential of IT within the English curriculum', *Journal of computer assisted learning* **6**(4).

Armitage, S. (1999) *Killing Time*. London: Faber.

Barnes, D. and Todd, F. (1977) *Communication and Learning in Small Groups*. London: Routledge and Keegan Paul.

Barnes, D. and Todd, F. (1995) *Communication and learning re-visited: Making meaning through talk*. Portsmouth, NH: Heinemann.

Brown, J. and Howlett, H. F. (1994) *Information technology works: Stimulate to educate*. Coventry: NCET.

Buckingham, D. and Sefton-Green, J. (1993) 'The interactive compact disc', *The English and Media Magazine*, Summer, no. 28.

Collins, J. (1993) 'Beyond the word processor: computer-mediated communications with pupils and teachers', *Computer Education* **73**. Computer Education Group and Schools Council Project Technology.

DES (1988) *Report of the Committee of Inquiry into the Teaching of English Language: The Kingman Report*. London: HMSO.

DfEE (1998) *National Literacy Strategy Framework for Teaching*. London: DfEE.

DfEE/QCA (2000) *The National Curriculum: Handbook for primary Teachers in England and Wales*. London: DfEE/QCA.

Hope, M. (1985) 'A new buzz word', *Times Educational Supplement*, 13 September.

Kuhn, S. and Stannard, R. (1997) *IT in English: Literature Review*. Coventry: NCET.

Lockwood, M. (1999) 'Opening the wardrobe of voices: standard English and language study at Key Stage 2', in Goodwin, P. (ed.) *The Literate Classroom*. London: David Fulton Publishers.

Mallett, M. and Newsome, B. (1977) *Talking, Writing and Learning 8–13*. London: Evans/Methuen.

Mercer, N. (1995) *The Guided Construction of Knowledge: talk amongst teachers and learners*. Clevedon: Multilingual Matters.

Mercer, N., Phillips, T. and Somekh, B. (1991) 'Research note: spoken language and new technology (SLANT)', *Journal of computer assisted Learning* **7**(3).

OFSTED (1999) *An Evaluation of the First Year of the NLS*. London: OFSTED.

Index